The Soul
Whence and Whither

The Soul
Whence and Whither

by Hazrat Inayat Khan

Sufi Order Publications
NEW LEBANON, NEW YORK
1977

SUFI ORDER PUBLICATIONS
P.O. Box 396
New Lebanon, New York 12125

Printed in the United States of America
ISBN 0-930872-00-2 (cloth), 0-930872-01-0 (paper)

NOTE ON PUBLICATION

The books published here were all originally edited from Hazrat Inayat Khan's lectures. *Akibat, Life After Death* and *The Phenomenon of the Soul* were both edited by Sherifa Lucy Goodenough as a part of the "Voice of Inayat" series, and were published in 1918 and 1919 respectively. *The Soul Whence and Whither* was prepared from lectures given during the Summer School at Suresnes, France, in 1923. Because the subject matter of these lecture series was somewhat similar, there is an occasional repetition of material. Rather than removing these repetitions, we have left the books as originally edited, only modernizing the spelling and punctuation.

Contents

Introduction

Sometime in the early Twenties, a group of people hailing from different lands sat spellbound in a garden in the suburbs of Paris, listening to an Eastern teacher. The teacher, Hazrat Inayat Khan, was talking, as from memory, of the experience of the soul as it descends from the night of time through the spheres. As he spoke, he reflected the mood, the attunement of the celestial beings he was talking about.

Was he reviving his listeners' own memories in the haze of the unconscious? Were they gleaning more from his being than from his words? What was said between the words? Some say they came back home transformed and exhilarated. Suddenly life fell into perspective; they had grasped a panoramic view in which their life fit into its place, rather than being caught in the narrow here and now of environment and fleeting events. No longer were they trapped by the accepted concepts of the universe reduced to its physical trappings, which had become, in the course of years, taken for granted. Hazrat Inayat Khan was helping his disciples to live meaningfully by making God present.

Pir Vilayat Inayat Khan

The Soul
Whence and Whither

Introduction

Before manifestation what existed? *Zat*, the truly existing, the only Being. In what form? In no form. As what? As nothing. The only definition that words can give is as the Absolute. In the Sufi terms this existence is termed *Ahadiat*. A consciousness arose out of the Absolute, the consciousness of existence. There was nothing of which the Absolute could be conscious, only of existence. This stage is called *wahdat*. Out of this consciousness of existence a sense developed, a sense "that *I* exist." It was a development of the consciousness of existence. It is this development which formed the first Ego, the Logos, which is termed *Wahdaniat* by the Sufis. With the feeling of the *I*-ness the innate power of the Absolute, so to speak, pulled itself together; in other words, concentrated on one point; thus the all-pervading radiance formed its center, the center which is the divine Spirit or the *Nur*, in Sufic terms called *Arwah*. This central Light then divided existence into two forms, light and darkness. In point of fact, there is no such thing as darkness; there has never been darkness; it is only more light compared with less light. This light and darkness formed *akasha* or *asman*, an accommodation, a mold; and the phenomenon of light and shade working through this mold furthered the manifestation into a great many accommodations, *asman*s or *akasha*s, one within the other. Every step manifestation has taken has resulted in a variety of forms made by the different substances which are produced during the process of spirit turning into matter. The working of this process has been according to the law of vibration, which is the secret of motion; and it is the plane of the definite forms of nature which is called in Sufic terminology *asman*. Out of these forms came gradually from the mineral the vegetable kingdom, and from the animal the human race, thus providing for the divine Spirit the *ajsaam*, the bodies which it has needed from the time it centered itself on one point, and from there spread its rays as various souls. Thus six definite steps towards manifestation are recognized by the Sufis. The first three are called *tanzi*, and the next three *tashbi*; the first three imperceptible, and the next three distinguishable.

There has been the phenomenon of four elements, besides one which is the source and goal of all elements, *nur*, the ether, making them five: *baad*, the air; *atesh*, the fire; *aab*, the water; *khaak*, the earth. These elements have worked in consonance with one another, in order to bring about the results desired by the divine Wisdom working behind them. In every *akasha* or *asman* they have been present more or less. One without the other did not exist; the four together brought the fifth. In this way the whole manifestation has taken place through a gradual process of development.

Manifestation finished half its task in the creation of man, in whom is born the wisdom of controlling and utilizing all that is on the earth to its best advantage. And in man the purpose of manifestation is fully accomplished, especially in such a man as has on his return journey become more and more conscious of the purpose by widening his outlook, and by living a fuller life; the man who has reached that stage of realization which is called divinity, in which is the fulfillment of the purpose of this whole manifestation.

Toward Manifestation

The divine Spirit is known by the mystics of all ages as the Sun; and therefore in all ancient mystical symbols the sun has been pictured as the sign of God. This conception gives a further help in the knowledge of metaphysics. The Sun is that aspect of the absolute God in which He begins to manifest, and the first step towards manifestation is contraction. That contraction is seen in all living beings and in all objects. It is first contraction that takes place, and next expansion, which comes as a matter of course, as a reaction; the former tendency is the desire of inhalation, and the latter exhalation. The contraction and expansion which is seen in all aspects of life comes from God Himself.

The omnipotent Light by this tendency becomes concentrated; and it is this concentrated light of Intelligence which is the Sun recognized by the mystics. As Shams-i Tabriz has said, "When the Sun of His countenance became manifest, the atoms of both worlds began to appear, as its light fell every atom donned a name and a form." The Hindus have called it in Vedanta *Chaitanya*, the Spirit or the Light of God. In the *Koran* it is mentioned, "We have made thy light out of Our Light, and of that light We have made the universe." In plain words, this explains that when there was nothing—no form, no name, no person, no object—there was Intelligence, and it is the contraction of that Intelligence which brought its essence into a form of Light which is called the divine Spirit; and the expression of the same Light has been the cause of the whole of manifestation.

Creation is the exhalation of God; and what is called destruction is absorption, which is the inhalation of God. The divine Spirit spreads itself; this we call creation, and it consists of various names and forms. There arises a conflicting condition or entanglement of the Breath of God, disorder in its rhythm, which manifests in destruction, and culminates in what is called by Hindus *pralaya*, the end of the world. For this many blame God, many judge Him, and many think it is unfair on the part of God to create and to destroy; but for God, Who is the only Being, this is the natural condition, by which He eternally lives. The beginning and the end of the world is only His one Breath, the duration of which is numberless years.

Between this one Breath myriads of beings have been born, have lived and died and experienced both this world and the next. Souls therefore are the rays of this Sun, which is called in Sanskrit *Brahma*. The nature of the ray is to extend and withdraw, to appear and disappear, and the duration of its existence is comparably short when compared with the duration of the eternal God, the divine Spirit. There are living creatures, small germs, worms and insects, who live no longer than a moment; and there are other beings whose life is of a hundred years, and some which live longer still; and yet it is a moment, even if it were a thousand years, compared with eternity. Time that man knows is in the first place discerned by the knowledge of his own physical constitution. From the Sanskrit word *pala*, which means moment, has come the word pulse—that which is pulsation. This knowledge has been completed to some extent by the study of nature, the changes of the seasons, and the journeys the world makes around the sun. Many wish to limit divine law to this man-made conception of time, and make speculations about it; but the tendency of the mystic is to bend his head low in worship as the thought of the eternal life of God, the only Being, comes to his mind. Instead of questioning why and what about it, he contemplates upon the being of God, and so raises his consciousness above the limitations of time and space, thus liberating his soul by lifting it to the divine spheres.

The soul, which is the ray of the divine Sun in one sphere, the sphere in which it does not touch any earthly being, is called *malak* or angel. Therefore every soul passes through the angelic heavens; in other words, every soul is an angel before it touches the earthly plane. It is the angels who become human beings; and those who do not become human beings, remain angels. The human being, therefore, is a grown-up angel; or an angel is a soul who has not grown sufficiently. Infants who come on earth with their angelic qualities, and sometimes pass away without having experienced the life of the grown-up man, show us the picture of the original condition of the soul. The idea that the angels are nearer to God is right according to this doctrine. Souls who have not journeyed farther are naturally close to the divine Spirit; they are angels.

Someone asked the Prophet why man was greater than the angels—man, who causes all the bloodshed on the earth, while the angels are always occupied in the praise of God. It is said in the Koran that the angels knew not anything of the earth; they knew God, and so they occupied themselves with God. But man is greater, for when he comes on earth he has much in the world to be occupied with, and still he pursues after God. That angelic sphere is pure from passions and emotions which are the source of all wrong and sin; souls pure of all greed and desires that the denseness of earth gives are angels who know nothing else but happiness, for happiness is the real nature of the soul.

The Hindus call the angels *suras*; *sura* means breath also, and breath means life. *Suras,* therefore, mean pure lives—lives that live long. In the Hindu scriptures there is another word used—*asura*, meaning lifeless; in other words, not in tune with the infinite. Man may continue to retain angelic qualities even in his life on the earth as a human being; and it is the angelic quality which can be traced in some souls who show innocence and sympathy in their lives. This is not necessarily weakness; it only shows the delicacy of a flower in the personality, together with fragrance.

Angelic souls on the earth plane are inclined to love, to be kind, to be dependent upon those who show them love. They are ready to believe, willing to learn, inclined to follow that which seems to them for the moment good, beautiful, and true. The picture of the angels that we read of in the Scriptures as sitting upon clouds and playing harps is but an expression of a mystical secret. Playing the harp is vibrating harmoniously; the angels have no actual harps, they themselves are the harps; they are living vibrations; they are life itself.

One can see in a person who is vibrating harmoniously that his presence becomes the inspiration of music and poetry. The person whose heart is tuned to the pitch of the angelic heavens will show on earth heavenly bliss; therefore the wise seek the association of spiritual beings. And sitting on clouds means that the angels are above all clouds; clouds are for the beings of the dense earth. They are free both from transitory pleasures and from the constant spells of depression; clouds do not surround them, for they are above clouds. Such souls, who are in direct touch with the Spirit of God, and who have no knowledge of the false world which is full of illusion, who live and know not death, whose lives are happiness, whose food is divine Light, make around *Arsh*, the divine Spirit, an aura which is called the highest heaven.

The souls in the angelic heavens have all goodness, and this shows that goodness is natural, and what is contrary to our nature we call evil. Souls in the angelic heavens are innocent; this also shows that innocence is the natural condition of the soul, and the lack of innocence is a foreign element, which the soul acquires after coming upon earth. In the angelic spheres the souls are happy; this shows that unhappiness does not belong to the soul. It is something which is foreign to it; therefore, in the experience of man, the discomfort coming out of life gives unhappiness. Souls on the earth have something of the angelic quality; therefore, they readily respond and are attracted without resistance to the innocence, happiness, and goodness of another person. If they knew that it is because this is the original quality of the soul they would develop the same in their own being. As Rumi has said, "People are drawn towards me, and they shed tears with my cries, and yet they know not what it is in me that attracts them."

Seeking after goodness, innocence, and happiness helps the angelic qualities to develop in a soul.

Spirituality, therefore, is the development of the angelic quality, and love of spirituality is the longing for the angelic heavens; it is homesickness.

Does death frighten the spiritual being? No, death for the spiritual soul is only a gate through which it enters into that sphere which every soul knows to be its home. Souls who become conscious of the angelic heavens, even in the smallest degrees, hear the call of that sphere; and if they have any discomfort in this world, it is that of the homesickness which the call of the angelic heavens gives. The soul may be likened to a ray of the sun; so the souls of the angels, being not adorned with a physical garb, are as flames themselves. The Scriptures therefore say that the angels are made of *nur* or light; *nur* is especially that light which comes from the divine Sun, the Spirit of God. All souls are made of that essence which is the essence of the whole manifestation; and the quality of that essence is that it absorbs all that is around it, and in time develops so that it will emerge into its own element, which is the divine.

The soul going towards manifestation which is still in the angelic heavens is free from all the differences and distinctions which are the conditions of the soul's life on earth. The dual aspect starts even from the angelic heavens. God alone is above duality; in all other conditions and aspects of life, this aspect is to be seen, though it is more distinct on the earth plane. In the angelic heavens it is not distinguishable.

People often question if the angels are in touch with those on earth, and the answer is that their life does not necessitate any communication with human life on earth, except in the case of some who are destined to perform a certain duty on the earth. It is mentioned in the ancient Scriptures that angels came with messages to the Prophets of Beni Israel; but the explanation of this from the metaphysical point of view is quite different from what an ordinary person would imagine. No man on earth is capable of communicating with the angels in heaven, nor is an angel from heaven inclined to communicate with man. But in the exceptional lives of the prophets what happens is that they rise above all the planes which keep man removed from the angelic heavens, and by doing so they are able to touch these heavens, and, being charged with the ever-glowing fire of inspiration from the angelic spheres where they come into touch with angels, they descend to the plane of the earth, and it is then that their words become tongues of flame, as spoken of in the Scriptures. This means that every word of theirs becomes a torch given into the hands of those who listen, to illuminate their hearts through life. Especially in the lives of the great ones who have given a divine message, a religion, to the world; their souls have never been discontented in any way with the angelic world, and it is this current, which linked their souls with the souls of the angels, that always kept them in contact with both heaven and earth.

The soul of the prophet, therefore, is a link between heaven and earth; it is a medium by which God's Message can be received. Then there are some spiritual souls who have had the experience in their lives of having been helped or warned by an angel. It is such souls who have kept a thread unbroken which they brought with them from the angelic world; they may be conscious of it or not, but there is a telegraphic wire which connects their souls with the souls of the angels, and they are conscious of having had contact with the angels.

Common disease is called normal health; when many cannot express something which is rare, they think the person who can experience such a thing has become mad. Therefore it is the law of the mystics to see all things, to experience all things, either of heaven or earth, and yet say little; for the souls incapable of understanding the possibility of their reach will ridicule them.

There is another aspect of the contact with the angels, and that is at the time of death. Many have seen in their lives the angels of death, but at the same time when death's call comes some have seen them in human form. Some have not seen them but have heard them speak. The reason is that there are some souls who have already departed from the earth plane, though the breath is still connecting the soul with the body, and such souls experience while still on the earth the angelic spheres at the time of their death. They see angels garbed in the form of their own imagination and hear the words of the angels in their own language. The reason is that it is necessary for a person who has lived on the earthly plane to clothe a being of the higher planes in earthly garments, and to interpret readily the language of the higher spheres in his own words. For instance, the angel Gabriel spoke to Moses in the Hebrew language, and to Mohammed in Arabic. One would ask, which was the language of the angel Gabriel, Arabic or Hebrew? Neither Arabic nor Hebrew was the language of Gabriel; his language was the language of the soul, and the soul knows the language of the soul. It is when a person interprets what he hears, even to himself, that he clothes the words he hears in his own language.

When the Spirit descended upon the twelve Apostles they began to speak all languages, and the meaning of this is that, when they were inspired by the angelic world, by the divine Sun or the Holy Ghost, they knew all languages; that is, they knew the language of the soul, which means that they heard before the men spoke to them. In other words, they were able to hear the voice of every soul through that inspiration. It would not give any special credit to the Apostles if one said they knew all the languages in the world instantly; for there are people even now to be found whose genius as linguists is so great that they know more than twenty or thirty languages. There is only one language which may be called "all languages," and that is the language of the soul. Before the illuminated soul all souls stand as written letters.

The guardian angel is a term known to many. This angelic protection comes to some souls on earth—souls who are walking on the earth and yet are linked in some way or other with the heavenly spheres. Often one sees an innocent child being saved from an accident; and often a person is warned to save a child at the moment when it is in danger. This guardian angel also appears in the same form as the angels sent to people on various duties.

There are recording angels, who take a record of our good and bad actions; and the most interesting thing is that those who keep the record of the good actions do not keep the record of the bad actions. Those who keep a record of the bad actions are other angels. And there is a further explanation given by the Prophet on this subject: that often a discussion takes place between those who keep the record of the good deeds and those who record the evil deeds. The former do not believe in the evil deeds because they are only conscious of man's goodness; they cannot believe that one who is good can be bad also. Also those who record the good points want their record to be filled and the other angels want their record to be filled, and so there is a great rivalry between them. Is this not the condition which we see in human nature? There is no person living on earth of whom all say good things; and there is no person living about whom all say bad things and no one says any good; and the most interesting point for a keen observer of life is how each tries to prove his argument to be correct.

In Sufi terms these two are called the angels of *khair* and of *khar*, and the difference in the spelling is very small. This suggests how little difference there is between goodness and badness. As Omar Khayyam says:

> A hair perhaps divides the false and true;
> Yes, and a single Alif were the clue,
> Could you but find it—to the treasure house,
> And, peradventure, to the Master too.

The ancient belief is that immediately after a dead person is buried these two kinds of angels come to his grave with their records and dispute about him. But do we not see in human nature the same thing? People do not even wait until after death; they begin to say things about the people they know, about their

friends and foes, and dispute about them even during their lifetime. The ancient belief was that after a dead person is put into
his grave and buried, two angels come to ask him questions, and
by this cross-examination to prove their arguments for and
against. Their names are Munkir and Nakir.

There is a story in the Bible that Jacob wrestled with an angel
all night; and before the breaking of the dawn Jacob won, and the
angel asked his name, blessed him, and gave him a new name.
The interpretation of this is that the illuminated souls of the angels
coming into contact with earthly beings are in conflict, and that
conflict ends when man has given up his earthly point of view
and has adopted the heavenly point of view. Then there is no more
a conflict but a blessing. And the asking of the name is a paradox,
for when once the false ego is crushed, the soul does not know
what its real name is; for the old name belongs to the false ego,
and he is given the true name, Israel, the great Name of God.

In reality there is only one kind of angel; but their relation with
human beings, and their desire to experience life through human
beings, divides them into nine degrees. Then there is a belief that
there are angels who are the inhabitants of heaven, and others
who live in the contrary place; those of the heaven are called
nur, light, and the others *nar*, which means fire in Arabic. This
is an extreme point of view; in reality, they can be distinguished
as two kinds, *jelal* and *jemal*, angels of power and angels of
beauty.

A question arises as to why the angels who descend on earth
as angels do not come as human beings, for every human being
was originally an angel. The angels who are related with human
beings are souls now in the angelic world, and they keep connection with human beings because of their wish; and now that
they have returned from the earthly regions to the angelic
heavens, they still keep in touch with the earth, either because of a
certain duty or because of their own pleasure.

The angelic spheres, the highest heavens, are the spheres of light which are called *nur*; and that current of power which runs through the divine Sun causes rays to spread, each ray being an angel or a soul. It is the divine current which, really speaking, is *nufs*, the breath or the ego. Breath is the ego, and ego is the breath. When the breath has left the body, the ego has gone. The nature of this current, which spreads as a ray and which is a life-current, is to collect and to create. It collects the atoms of the sphere in which it is running, and it creates out of itself all that it can create. Therefore in the angelic heavens, which is the sphere of radiance, the soul collects the atoms of radiance. A Sufi poet of Persia has given a most beautiful expression of this idea in a verse: "A glow garbed with a flame came." Before the angels were conceived by artists in the form of human beings, they were symbolized as burning lamps; from this comes the custom of lighting candles in religious services, showing thereby to some extent what the angels were like before they became human souls.

In the ancient Scriptures it is mentioned that human beings produced by their virtues angels. This is only a symbological expression; it is not that human beings produced angels by their virtues, but that their virtues lifted their souls to the angels. One may ask, if the souls who have settled in the angelic heavens are angels, then what makes them come to the earth? The answer is that it is not the angels who have settled in the angelic heavens who come to the earth, for these rays have finished their creative power in manifesting as angels. If they had a greater power they would certainly have gone farther, even to the physical plane, and would have preferably manifested as human beings; for the desire of every soul is to reach the ultimate culmination in manifestation, and that culmination is the stage of the human plane.

It is the work of the souls who return from the earth to communicate with the earth very often, and it is such angels who are generally known to man. Angels who have never manifested as men on earth, if they ever experience life on the earth, only experience it by the medium of other minds and bodies, which by their evolution come closer to the angelic heavens. They take these as their instruments, and at times reflect themselves in them, and at times have them reflected in themselves. This is not obsession but inspiration.

Souls in the angelic heavens live as a breath. The soul in its nature is a current, a current the nature of which is to envelop itself with all that may come along and meet it on its way. The soul collects all that comes to it, therefore it becomes different from its original condition; yet in its real being the soul is a vibration, the soul is a breath, the soul is intelligence, and the soul is the essence of the personality. The question very often arises, if an angel comes from above, does it descend outwardly before a person or manifest within a person in the heart?

The "lift" which brings a soul down and takes it back to heaven is situated within; that "lift" is the breath; the soul comes to earth with the breath, and with the same it returns. Those among human beings who are not even aware of their own breath, how can they know who comes within themselves and who goes out? Many seem wide awake to the life without but asleep to the life within; and though the chamber of their heart is continually visited by the Hosts of Heaven, they do not know their own heart; they are not there.

There is a very interesting story told in the Arabic Scriptures. It is that God made Iblis the chief among the angels and then told him to bring some clay that He might make out of it an image. The angels, under the direction of Iblis, brought the clay and made an image; then God breathed into that image and asked the angels to bow before it. All the angels bowed; but Iblis said, "Lord, Thou hast made me the chief of all angels, and I have brought this clay at Thy command, and made with my own hands this image which Thou commandest me to bow before." The displeasure of God arose and fell on his neck as the sign of the outcast.

This story helps us to understand what Jesus Christ meant when he said, "Blessed are the meek, for they shall inherit the earth." What Iblis denied was the reflection of God in man; and one can observe the same law in every direction of life. A person may be rich in wealth or high in position, but he still must obey the policeman. It is not the rank and wealth which the latter has, but in him is reflected the power of the government, and when a man takes no heed of the policeman, he refuses to obey the law of the state. In everything small or great it is the same law; and in every person there is a spark of this tendency of Iblis, the tendency which we know as egotism, the tendency of saying, no, I will not listen, I will not give in, I will not consider. Because of what? Because of "I"; because "I am." But there is only one "I"—the *Perfect I.* He is God, whose power is mightier than any power existing in the world, whose position is greater than that of anyone; and He shows it in answer to the egotistic tendency of man, who is limited. This is expressed in the saying, "Man proposes, but God disposes." It is this thought which teaches man the virtue of resignation, which shows him that the *I* he creates is a much smaller *I*, and that there is no comparison between this *I* and the *I* of the great Ego, God.

Another story tells how frightened the soul was when it was commanded to enter the body of clay; it was most unwilling, not from pride, but from fear. The soul, whose nature is freedom, whose dwelling place is heaven, whose comfort it is to be free and to dwell in all the spheres of existence—for that soul to dwell in a house made of clay was most horrifying. Then God asked the angels to play and sing, and the ecstasy that was produced in the soul by hearing that music made it enter the body of clay, where it became captive to death. The interpretation of this idea is that the soul, which is pure intelligence and angelic in its being, had not the least interest in dwelling in the physical plane, which robs it of its freedom and makes it limited; but what interested the soul and made it come into the body is what this physical world offers to the senses, and this produces such an intoxication that it takes away for the moment the thought of heaven from the soul, and so the soul becomes captive in the physical body. What is Cupid? Is not Cupid the soul? It is the soul: the angel going towards manifestation, the angel which has arrived at its destination, the human plane; and before it manifests there it is Cupid.

The soul which has passed through the angelic heavens in its descent to earth comes next to the sphere of the *djinn*, or *genius*. This is the sphere of mind and may be called the spiritual sphere, for it is mind and soul which make spirit. The souls who halt in this sphere, being attracted by its beauty, settle there; also the souls who have no power to go farther into outer manifestation become the inhabitants of this sphere. Therefore there are three kinds of souls who touch this sphere on their way to manifestation: the souls who are attracted to this sphere, and who desire to remain there; the souls who are unable to go farther, and who have to settle there; and the souls who are continuing their journey towards the earth plane, and who are on their way to the earth through this plane.

The genius is an entity with a mind, but not such a mind as that of man; a mind more pure, more clear, and which is illuminated by the light of Intelligence. The mind of the genius is deeper in perception and in conception, because it is empty, not filled with thoughts and imaginations as is that of man. It is the mind of the genius which may be called the "empty cup"—a cup into which knowledge can be poured, in which there is accommodation. It is for this reason that the teachers on the spiritual path appreciate the quality of the genius in the mind of their pupils, in which they find accommodation for knowledge. A cup which is already filled, or even partly filled, does not give free accommodation for that knowledge which the teacher wishes to pour into the heart of his pupil. As the genii are keen in perception and conception, so they are keen in expression either in word or deed. The action of the genius extends as far as the mind can reach; and the word of the genius reaches even farther than the voice, for it takes as its root the mental sphere which is above the air-waves.

The genius comes closer to man than the angel, for in the genius there is something like the mind which is completed in man. All the intuitive and inspirational properties are possessed by the genius, because that is the only source that the genius has of receiving its knowledge. Subjects such as poetry, music, art, inventive science, philosophy, and morals are akin to the nature of the genius. The artist, the poet, the musician, and the philosopher show in their gifts throughout their lives the heritage of the genius. The word *genius* comes from a Sanskrit word *gryana*, which means knowledge. The genii, therefore, are the beings of knowledge, whose hunger is for knowledge, whose joy is in learning, in understanding, and whose work is in inspiring, and bringing light and joy to others. In every kind of knowledge that exists, the favorite knowledge to a genius is the knowledge of truth, in which is the fulfillment of its life's purpose.

The sphere of the genius is the universe of minds. It may be called a mental world; and yet the soul is with the mind. The soul with the mind is called spirit, and therefore it may also be called a spiritual world. The questions, what are the genii like?, what do they look like?, may be answered in the same way as in explaining the forms of angels: that things are not always as they are, but as we see them. Man always pictures the beings he imagines and cannot see with his physical eyes as something like himself, or man's imagination may gather together different forms—for instance, wings from birds, horns from oxen, hooves from horses, and paws from tigers. He puts them all together and makes a new form.

It is beyond possibility to exactly explain what the genius looks like, and yet there is no being who lives without a form. In support of man's imagination, which pictures the angel or genius more or less in the form of man, there is much that can be said. For everything in the world proves at the end of examination that it is striving to culminate into the form of man. Rocks, trees, fruits, flowers, mountains, and clouds all show a gradual development towards the image of man. A keen observer of nature will prove this a thousand times; there is everything in the world to support this argument. Every form shows either a part of the human form or an undeveloped outline of it. As it is with material things and with the lower creation, so in the same way it is towards the human form that even the form of the genius and the angel is growing. It is this idea which is spoken of in the Scriptures in the words, "We have made man in our own image." If I were to add a word of explanation I would say, "We have made all forms in order to complete the image of man."

The world of the genii is the world of minds, yet the minds of the genii are not so developed as the minds of men. The reason for this is that the experience of life on the earth completes the making of mind. In the world of the genii the mind is only a design, an outline, a design which is not yet embroidered. What is the occupation of the genii? What does the world of the genii look like? One may give a thousand explanations, but nothing can explain it fully. For instance, if a person were to ask me what

China looks like, I would say, "Most wonderful, most interesting"; but if he said, "What is wonderful in China?" I would say, "Go and take a tour through China in order that you may see it fully."

We have not sufficient words to explain what the genius is like, or what the world of the genius is; but what little can be said about it is that it is a world of music, art, poetry, a world of intelligence, cheerfulness and joy, a world of thought, imagination and sentiment, a world that a poet would long for and a musician would crave to dwell in. The life of the genius is an ideal life for a thinker; a life which is free from all illness, pure from all bitterness of human nature, free to move about in space without any hindrance; a most joyful place, where the Sun of Intelligence shines, where the trouble of life and death is not so serious, life not so short as on the earth. If there is any paradise it is the world of the genius. Hindus have called it *Indra-loka*, and picture *Gandharva*s and *Upsara*s to be there; a paradise of which every prophet has spoken to his followers in the way in which they could understand it. The question, how does a prophet know of this, may be answered by saying that the soul of the prophet is like a fruit which by its weight touches the ground; it has not dropped on to the earth like other fruits; it is still connected with the branch to which it is attached, the branch which droops through all the planes of existence; and so he, in his experience of the different planes, so to speak, touches all worlds. It is this mystery which is hidden behind the life of the prophet. It is through this branch that the fruit is connected with the stem; therefore, though on earth, he calls aloud the name of God. While to many God is an imagination, to him God is the reality.

The soul is a current. We may call it an electric current, yet one unlike the electric current we know on this physical plane, different from it in its power and phenomena: a current which runs more speedily than anything we know; a current which is beyond time and space; a current which runs through all the planes of life. If manifestation is the Breath of God, according to the conception of the yogi, there is one Breath and there are many breaths. The one Breath, which is the central breath, is called by Yogis *prana*, and all other breaths which have a certain part to play in the mechanism of the human body are lesser breaths; and again *prana* and all other breaths, when put together make one Breath, which man calls life. Souls, therefore, are different breaths of God. This idea may be pictured as a tree which has a stem and various branches, each branch in its place representing a stem.

The elements of every sphere are different. Just as the air of every part of the world is different, the water is different, and the earth of every part of the world in its effect upon the human being is different, so the atoms of every plane are different; their nature and character are as different as their effect. Therefore the form of the angel need not be compared in any way with the form of the genius; neither can the form of the genius be compared with the form of man, for the atoms of which the genius is made belong to another sphere. A man who is accustomed to physical forms cannot very well grasp the idea of the forms of the genii. This shows us that the soul shoots forth and functions in a body which that particular sphere offers it. The heavens, for instance, offer that luminous body to the soul, which in the Sufic term is called *nur*, because heaven consists of luminous atoms—it is all illumination. It is the recognition of that angelic body in the Buddha which caused his disciples to make the statue of Buddha in gold. Often artists have had the conception of painting angels in gold, for gold represents light.

The soul that goes as far as the sphere of the genius as a current coming from the heavens functions in a body of the sphere of genius. The question is, a soul which comes from the heavens through the world of angels, does it come to the world of the genii without a body? It comes with a body, the angelic body; yet it becomes necessary for the soul coming with the angelic body into the world of genii to adopt a body of that particular world in order to withstand the weather of that plane. Animals which live in cold countries have a different skin from those that live in a tropical climate. That is the condition for going into any other sphere. Even if a person were journeying, going from a tropical country to another tropical country, and on the way he had to pass through a cold climate, he would need suitable garments for that climate. The body is a garment of the soul; the soul wears this garment in order to stand the conditions of that particular sphere.

Souls which are passing through the sphere of the genii towards the physical plane, and who do not stop in that sphere, meet with other travellers who are on their journey back home, and they learn from them a great many things. There is "give and take," there is buying and selling, there is learning and teaching; but who teaches the most? The one with most experience, the one who is going back home. This latter gives the map of the journey to the soul travelling towards manifestation. It is from this map that the travelling soul strikes his path rightly or wrongly. One soul may have one kind of instruction, another soul may have another kind; one soul may be clear, another may be confused. Yet they all go forward as the travellers of a caravan, taking with them all the precious information, all the things which they have learned from the others on the journey. It is for this reason that every child born on earth possesses, besides what he has inherited from his parents and ancestors, a power and knowledge quite peculiar to himself and different to that which his parents and ancestors possessed; yet he knows not whence he received it, or who gave him the knowledge; but he shows from the beginning of his life on earth signs of having known things which he has never been taught. One soul is more impressionable than another. One soul is perhaps more impressed by the angelic heavens, and that impression has remained more deeply with it throughout the whole journey. Another is more impressed by the sphere of the genii, and that impression lasts through the whole journey. Then there is another soul who is not deeply impressed with the angelic heavens or the world of the genius, and that soul does not know of these worlds; he comes through blindly, and is only interested in things of the earth when he reaches it. One finds generally among artists, poets, musicians, thinkers, as well as among philosophers, great politicians, and inventors, souls of the world of the genii, who have brought with them on to the earth some deep impression which proves them in their lives to be what men term great "geniuses."

Impression is a great phenomenon in itself. "As a man thinketh, so is he!" And what does man think? He thinks of that with which he is most impressed; and what he is most impressed with, that he himself is. Do we not see in our life on earth that people who are deeply impressed with a certain personality, wish, thought, or feeling become in time the same? If this is true, what is man? Man is his impression. The soul impressed deeply in the world of the genii by some personality coming back from the earth, an impression deeply engraved upon that soul which it can never throw away, certainly becomes that personality itself with which it is impressed. Suppose a soul is impressed in the world of the genius with the personality of Beethoven; when born on earth he is Beethoven in thought, feeling, tendency, inclination, and knowledge; only in addition to that personality he has the heritage of his parents and of his ancestors. As the son of a certain family is called by the name of that family, so the impression of a certain personality may rightfully be called by that name. Therefore if

Shankaracharya claims to be the reincarnation of Krishna, there is every reason for his claim, as this theory stands in support of it.

Life from the beginning to the end is a mystery. The deeper one dives in order to investigate the truth, the more difficulty one finds in distinguishing what is called individuality. But it is not the aim of the wise to hold on to individuality. Wisdom lies in understanding the secret of individuality, its composition, or its decomposition, which resolves in the end into one individuality, the individuality of God. As it is written, "There is one God; none exists save He."

Souls who are impressed in the world of the genius by the personalities of those they meet on their way towards manifestation receive different kinds of impressions. Some are deeply impressed by one personality, and some are slightly impressed by one personality. Some souls receive many impressions on that plane, and it is hardly distinguishable which impression has more effect and which less. However, it is certainly true that in reality one impression is predominant in every soul. The soul, so to speak, conceives this impression, an impression which is not only the outline of the personality which impresses it, but is the very essence of the personality. A soul may not be compared with an object, for the soul is all the life there is; therefore it not only takes an impression like a photographic plate, but it becomes nurtured by it. The soul is creation, therefore it expresses all that it has absorbed on its way.

The question, is a genius sent on earth on a mission to human beings, may be answered, that whether angel, genius, or man, all are intended to play their part in the scheme of working of the whole universe, and all are used by the Wisdom of God for the purpose for which they were created. No doubt the angels are primarily for the angelic heavens and the genii for the sphere of the genius, yet in a house the inhabitants of the second or third floor are sometimes sent to the ground floor on an errand when it is necessary.

The most remarkable thing that one notices in all those planes of existence is that the beings of these separate planes are not imprisoned there by the Creator. They become captive themselves, just as a man who lives in a village passes his whole life in the same place, and when he is told of the history of the neighboring county it is for him as another world. He never tries to leave his village, and the neighboring county is foreign to him. He has heard the name of the next village all through his life, but he has never made it possibile to visit it. It is this nature of the soul which arises from its ignorance that limits that which is, in point of fact, limitless.

How does the soul of a genius communicate with human beings on earth? It focuses itself upon the heart of man, and experiences all that the man experiences, and knows all that the man knows. It is easy for a genius to do this, because its mind is clear like crystal, and it can accommodate and reflect all that falls within its range of vision. One might ask, if the souls on their return journey from the earth give their experience to the souls coming from above, what do the souls coming from above give to the souls on their return journey? They can do a great deal, too; for they know the "forgotten ways" through which they have recently travelled, and the laws and customs of the way that the souls on the return journey need to learn. Besides this they give to them that light and life which is necessary to those worn out and withered souls who have probably given most of themselves to the ever-robbing and consuming plane of the earth. In this way a man is helped onwards towards his goal by the soul he meets on the way in his own return journey.

The question, in what manner can the genii help man on the earth, may be answered by saying that they are capable of inspiring man, not with a definite knowledge of things, but with the sense of the knowledge, especially of the knowledge of art, beauty, tone, and rhythm; knowledge of the inventive nature, and sometimes with a sense of knowledge that might help to accomplish great things in life. But though they meet as inhabitants of different countries who know not the language, it is the language of the heart which becomes the medium of communication. Heart talks to heart, and soul speaks to soul.

Manifestation

After the soul has passed through the sphere of the genii, it arrives on the physical plane. What helps this soul to come on to the physical plane? What opens the way for this new-coming soul to enter physical existence? The coming soul enters the physical sphere by the channel of the breath. Breath is the power at the back of every action. It works as a battery which keeps the physical mechanism of the human body going. The secret of birth and death is to be found in the mystery of the breath.

What is Cupid? It is the soul which is being born. Before it appears on the physical plane it is pictured by the wise as a Cupid or angel; it is an angel, for the soul itself is the angel. Duality in every aspect of life, and on whatever plane, is creative, and its issue is the purpose and the outcome of the dual aspect of nature. The affinity which brings about the fulfillment of the purpose is the power of Cupid; in reality it is the phenomenon of the soul.

When the soul is born on earth its first expression is a cry. Why does it cry? Because it finds itself in a new place which is all strange to it. It finds itself in captivity, which it has not experienced before. Every person, every object is new and is something foreign to this soul. But soon this condition passes away. Soon the senses of the infant become acquainted with the outer life which so continually attracts its attention. It first becomes interested in breathing the air of the world, then in hearing the sounds, and then in seeing the objects before it, then in touching them, and then its taste develops. The more familiar the soul becomes with this physical world the more interested it becomes, though sometimes it shows homesickness in the fits of crying that it so often has during its infancy. It is not always illness; it is not always that it is crying for things outside. No doubt as it grows it longs for things outside itself; but it often cries from the feeling of having been removed from a place which was more pleasant and comfortable, and having come to a foreign land of which it knows so little. It is this which causes the infant to have fits of crying.

The wisdom of nature is perfect; and there is no better vision of the splendour of the divine Wisdom for the thinker than an infant in its early infancy. If the senses of an infant were developed, as are the senses of the grown-up person, it would have lost its reason from the sudden pressure of the physical world falling instantly upon it. Its delicate senses would not have been able to stand the pressure of so many and various and intense activities of this world. How marvellously works the Wisdom behind, which is the evidence of the divine Protector, Father, Mother, Creator, the support and protection of all, so that the sense of the child develops gradually as it becomes more familiar with life. The more it knows the more its mind expands; and it cannot know more than its mind can grasp. So that in every way an infant is protected in both mind and body.

When the soul comes into the physical world it receives an offering from the whole universe, and that offering is the body in which to function. It is not offered to the soul only by the parents, but by the ancestors, by the nation and race into which the soul is born, and by the whole human race. This body is not only an offering of the human race, but is an outcome of something that the whole world has produced for ages: a clay which has been kneaded a thousand times over; a clay which has been prepared so that in its very development it has become more intelligent, more radiant, and more living; a clay which appeared first in the mineral kingdom, which developed in the vegetable kingdom, which then appeared as the animal, and which was finished in the making of that body which is offered to the new-coming human soul. One may ask, is it not true, then, as some scientists say in their biological study, that man has risen from the animal kingdom? Certainly it is true, but true in the sense explained above.

We need not understand by this that every rock turned into a plant, and every plant into an animal, and every animal into a man. The soul is direct from heaven; it functions in a body, and it is this body through which it experiences life on the earth more fully. Rocks, trees, and animals, therefore, may not be considered as the ancestors of the soul. It is the body which is the outcome of the working of all these different kingdoms, which are the development of one another.

A question arises, why must a soul function in a human body? Why not in an animal, bird, or insect? The answer is that it does so function. Every soul is not the same ray, has not the same illumination, the same far-reaching power, or the same volume; and therefore it is true that souls do not only function in a human body, but in all forms, however insignificant and small. What about rocks, mountains, seas, and rivers? Are they not the outcome of the soul? The answer is that nature in general in its various aspects is the naturalization of that Light which is called divine Spirit; but not everything in nature has what man understands by *soul*, for he recognizes only that ray which functions in the human body as a soul. He does not recognize the ray which functions in the lower creation to be the same, although it comes from the same source. There are two things: there are the rays, and there is Light from which they spring. If the rays are the source of the soul of human beings, then the Light of that same divine Sun is the Spirit of the whole of nature. It is the same Light, but not divided, not distinct, as are the rays which we call souls.

Why has nature its different aspects? If the Spirit behind it is one, why is everything in nature separate and different? The answer is that creation is a gradual evolution of that Light which is the source and goal of all beings. For instance, plant life is a development of the mineral kingdom, animal life of the vegetable kingdom, and human life the culmination of this evolution. But this culmination is the finishing of that vehicle which the soul uses. By this evolution the soul is not evolved; by this evolution is only meant that the soul has adopted a more finished instrument in order to experience life more fully. No doubt the better the instrument the greater the satisfaction of the soul. When one looks from this point of view at the whole creation one feels it to be the truth that not only man, but the whole of manifestation, was created in the image of God.

The soul, which has already brought with it from the angelic heavens a luminous body, from the sphere of the genius a body full of impressions, functions in the end in the human body, which the physical plane offers it, and it settles for some time in this abode. This completes what we understand by the word *individuality*. These three planes, which are the principal planes of existence, are called in the terms of Vedanta: *bhu-loka, deva-loka, svar-loka,* meaning three worlds: *bhu-loka* the physical world, *deva-loka* the world of the genii, and *svar-loka* the world of the angels. The human being therefore has all three beings in him—the angel, the genius, and man.

What man acquires on the earth is the experience which he has gained by the means of his senses, an experience which he himself undergoes, and it is this experience which man collects in that accommodation within himself which he calls the heart. The surface of the heart, which is the collection of his knowledge, he calls the mind. This word comes from the Sanskrit *manas*, mind, and from this the word *man* has come. Man shows the signs of the angelic heavens and the sphere of the genius by his tendencies, his tendency for light, truth, love, and righteousness; his love of God; his seeking for the truth of life; this all shows the angel in him. In his longing for beauty, in his drawing towards art, in his love for music, in his appreciation of poetry, in his tendency to produce, to create, to express, he shows signs of the sphere of the genius. The impressions which constitute his being, which he has brought as a heritage from the sphere of the genius, which have been imparted to him by the souls on their way back towards the goal, he shows also as something peculiar and different to what his people possess.

No doubt it often happens that a child possesses qualities of his ancestors which were perhaps missing in his parents, or even two or three generations back; however, this is another heritage, a heritage which is known to us as such. I might express this by saying that a soul borrows a property from the spheres of the genius, and a more concrete property from the physical world; and, as it borrows this property, together with this transaction it takes upon itself the taxation and the obligations as well as the responsibilities which are attached to the property. Very often the property is not in proper repair, and damage has been done to it, and it falls to his lot to repair it; and if there be a mortgage on that property, that becomes his due. Together with the property, he becomes the owner of the records and the contracts of the property which he owns. In this is to be found the secret of what is called *karma*.

What makes the soul know of its own existence? Something with with it adorns itself, something which it adopts, possesses, owns, and uses. For instance, what makes a king know that he is a king? His palace, his kingly environment, people standing before him in attendance; if all that were absent, the soul would be no king. Therefore the king is a palace, and it is the consciousness of the environment which makes the soul feel, "I am so and so." What it adorns itself with makes it say, "I am this or that." Otherwise by origin it is something nameless, formless. On the earth plane the personality develops out of the individuality. The soul is an individual from the moment it is born upon the earth in the worldly sense of the word; but it becomes a person as it grows, for personality is the development of individuality; and in personality, which is built by character-building, is born that spirit which is the rebirth of the soul. The first birth is the birth of man, the second birth is the birth of God.

The law that governs the soul's manifestation may be divided into three parts:

1. That of the angelic heavens.
2. That of the sphere of the genius.
3. That of the world of man, or the physical plane.

In the angelic heavens there are no distinct impressions, but there is a tuning. The soul is tuned to a certain pitch by the law of vibration, high or low according to the impression it receives from the souls coming back home. In this tuning it gets, so to speak, a tone and rhythm which directs its path towards the world of the genius. Souls in themselves are not different in the angelic heavens, as they are immediately next to that of the divine Being. If there is a difference of souls in the angelic heavens, it is the difference of more or less radiance, and a longer or a shorter scope of their range.

That which attracts souls from the sphere of the genius to the human world is what they receive from the souls who are homeward bound. In accordance with this they take their direction towards the physical world. If I were to give this idea in a more expressive form, I would say it is like a person whose heart is tuned to love and light, and to appreciate and to admire beauty. He will certainly take a direction towards a greater beauty, and will seek such friends to meet with and learn from as seem to him in some way similar to his nature or ideal. This is an example of the soul which is attracted from the angelic heavens to the sphere of the genius. A person who has studied music and practiced through his life will certainly seek the association of musical friends, artists, singers, composers, and lovers of music. Among these he will find his friends, his comrades; and so a soul from the sphere of the genius is directed according to its love for certain things to find those things on the physical plane. This shows that God does not thrust certain conditions upon the souls going towards manifestation, but in this manner they choose them.

A person may say, "But no soul can have chosen for itself miserable conditions!" The answer to this we find before us in this world. Many here cause their own miseries; they may not know it, they may not admit it, nevertheless many of man's joys and sorrows are caused by himself. By this is not meant that this is the only law that governs life. This is a law in answer to the question that rises out of common sense, but if one raised one's head from this world of illusion and looked up and asked God, "Tell me the secret and the mystery of Thy Creation," one would hear in answer that every thing and being is placed in its own place, and each is busy carrying out that work which has to be done in the whole scheme of nature. Life is a symphony; and the action of every person in this symphony is the playing of his particular part in the music.

When the war was going on all people were called to arms, and were placed, regardless of their profession, qualifications, or moral standard, in places where they were needed; the reason

was that the "Call of the Purpose" was to be the first consider-
ation. If there is anything which will bring peace to the thinker it
is the understanding of this. The thought, "I am suffering now
because of my sins in a past life," may bring an answer to the
inquiring and reasoning mind and stop it from rebelling for the
moment, but will this take away the irritation that the misery is
causing in the heart? Will that mind ever excuse God for having
so severely judged him? He may own his mistakes of the past, but
will he ever believe in God as a God of love and compassion, as
a God of mercy, or as a God of forgiveness?

The soul comes on earth, rich or poor, ripened or unripened,
through three phases where it has either enriched or lost its
opportunity. It takes light from the angelic heavens, knowledge
from the sphere of the genius, and it inherits qualities from its
parents and ancestors on the earth plane.

Of the things that it has collected on its way to manifestation
on the earth it has made that accommodation which is called the
mind. The body in which the soul functions on the physical plane
also contributes to the soul the properties of all the worlds to which
it has belonged: the mineral, the vegetable, and the animal kingdoms. It is for this reason that man is called a universe in himself;
for man consists in himself of all that is in heaven and all that is on
earth. "We have made him Our Khalif," says God in the Koran,
referring to man; meaning Our representative, Our chief, into
whose care a universe is given. Man verily is himself the universe.

Man shows in his life traces of all the conditions through which
the clay that makes his body has gone. There are atoms of his
body which represent the mineral kingdom, the vegetable kingdom, and the animal kingdom; all these are represented in him.
Not only his body but his mind shows the reflection of all the
kingdoms through which it has passed, for the mind is the medium
between heaven and earth. Man experiences heaven when

conscious of his soul; he experiences the earth when conscious of his body. Man experiences that plane which is between heaven and earth when he is conscious of his mind. Man shows by his stupidity the mineral kingdom which is in him, thick and hard; he shows by his pliability the vegetable kingdom, by his productive and creative faculties which bring forth the flowers and fruits of his life from his thoughts and deeds; he shows the traces of the animal kingdom in him by his passions, emotions, and attachments, by his willingness for service and usefulness. And if one were to say what represents the human in him, the answer is all things, all the attributes of earth and heaven—the stillness, the hardness, and strength of the stone; the fighting nature, the tendency to attachment from the animals; the fruitfulness and usefulness of the vegetable kingdom; the inventive, artistic, poetical, and musical genius of the sphere of the genius; the beauty, illumination, love, calm, and peace of the angelic planes— all these things put together make man. It is therefore that the human soul consists of all, and thus culminates into that purpose for which the whole creation has taken place.

The soul manifested on the earth is not at all disconnected with the higher spheres. It lives in all spheres, but knows mostly one sphere, ignorant of the others, on which it turns its back. Thus the soul becomes deprived of the heavenly bliss, and conscious of the troubles and limitations of life on the earth. It is not the truth that Adam was put out of the Garden of Eden; he only turned his back on it, which made him an exile from heaven. The souls of seers, saints, masters, and prophets are conscious of the different spheres. It is therefore that they are connected with the worlds of the angels and genii, and with the Spirit of God. The condition of the one becomes like that of a captive imprisoned on the ground floor of the house: he has no access to the other floors of the building wherever he may wish to dwell.

The secret of life is that every soul by its nature is *asman* or *akasha*, an accommodation, and has in it an appetite; and of all that it partakes it creates a cover which surrounds it as a shell, and the life of that shell becomes dependent upon the same substance of which it is made. Therefore the shell becomes susceptible to all influences, and subject to the laws of that sphere from which it seeks its sustenance, or rather, the sustenance of the shell. The soul cannot see itself; it sees what is around it, it sees that in which it functions; and so it enjoys the comforts of the shell which is around it, and experiences the pains and discomforts which belong to the shell; and in this way it becomes an exile from its birth land, which is the Being of God, which is divine Spirit; and it seeks consciously or unconsciously once again the peace and happiness of home. God, therefore, is not the goal but the abode of the soul—its real Self, its true Being.

There are five spheres of which the soul is capable of being conscious. What are these spheres? These spheres are the different shells, each shell having its own work. The first sphere of which man becomes conscious after his birth on earth is *nasut*, a sphere which is commonly known as the physical plane. How are the comforts and discomforts of this sphere experienced? By the medium of the physical body, and when there is something wrong with an organ of the senses the soul is deprived of that particular experience that it would like to have on this physical plane. The physical body is susceptible to all changes of climate and becomes dependent in its experience and expression, thus making the soul dependent and limited. Therefore, with all the riches that the world can give, man, who is only conscious of this sphere, is limited. "God alone is rich, and all souls living on earth are poor" (Koran).

Malakut is the next sphere, the sphere of thought and imagination, where there is a greater freedom and less limitation than one experiences on the physical plane. A man with thought and imagination can add to life that comfort and beauty which is lasting on the physical plane. And the more real his imagination becomes the more conscious of that sphere of mind he proves to be. This sphere of mind is his world, not smaller than this world, but much larger—a world which can accommodate all that the universe holds, and yet there would be a place in it to be filled.

The third sphere is *djabrut*, a sphere of the soul in which the soul is at home. In the waking state the soul of the average man only touches this sphere for a moment at a time. Man does not know where he is at that moment. He calls it abstraction. Do they not say, when a person is not listening, that he is not here? Every soul is lifted up to that sphere, even if it be for only a moment, and with the life and light with which the soul is charged in that sphere the soul is enabled to live on this earth the life full of struggles and difficulties. Nothing in the world could give man the strength that is needed to live a life on the earth if there were no blessings from heaven reaching him from time to time, of which he is so little aware.

The other two spheres are experienced in sleep, but they are not different spheres; they are only different because they are experienced in sleep. They are *malakut*, which is experienced in dreams, the world of mind, of thought and imagination; and *djabrut*, the state of deep sleep when even the mind is still—a sleep which frees the suffering patient from pain, and gives to the prisoner freedom from his prison; that state of sleep which takes away from the mind its load of worry and anxiety, and removes from the body every exhaustion and tiredness, bringing to mind and body repose, rest, and peace, so that after man has wakened from his deep sleep he feels comfortable, rested, invigorated, as if a new life had come to him. One would give anything in the world to have a deep sleep, though so few know its value. That state of *malakut* is reached while in the waking state by the great thinkers, the great inventive minds and the gifted artists, and is experienced by the seers and sages. It is to experience this that all the concentrations are given by spiritual teachers to their disciples. This fuller experience is also called *lahut*.

Still another experience is *hahut*, a further stage, which is experienced by souls who have attained the most high spiritual attainment, which is called *samadhi* in Vedantic terms. In this experience a person is conscious of *djabrut* while awake; and this state he brings about at will.

Though for the sake of experience these spheres are explained as five spheres, yet chiefly they are three—*nasut*, the plane of the world of man; *malakut*, the sphere of the genius; and *djabrut*, the angelic world.

Now there is a question if a soul by rising to all these spheres becomes conscious of the sphere of the genius and of the angelic heavens, or if it only sees within itself its self-made world of mind, and the spheres of joy and peace within itself. The answer is, first it sees its own world by rising to the sphere called *malakut*. It experiences the joy and peace which belong to its own heart, and which are of its own being. But that is one part of spiritual attainment. This part of the attainment is the way of the Yogi. The way in which the Sufi differs from the Yogi is in his expansion; and it is these two sides of the journey which are pictured by the two lines of the cross, the perpendicular and the horizontal. The perpendicular line shows a progress straight within from *nasut* to *djabrut*, experiencing one's own world within oneself; but that which the horizontal line denotes is expansion. The Sufi therefore tries to expand as he goes on progressing, for it is the largeness of the soul which will accommodate all experiences and in the end will become God-conscious and all-embracing. The man who shuts himself up from all men,

however high spiritually he may be, he will not be free in *malakut*
—in the higher sphere. He will have a wall around him, keeping
away the genius and even the angels of the angelic heavens; and
so his journey will be exclusive. It is therefore that Sufism does not
only teach concentration and meditation, which help one to make
one-sided progress, but the love of God which is expansion; the
opening of the heart to all beings, which is the way of Christ and
the sign of the cross.

Every person shows from his earthly heritage a nature that
divides men into four classes:

The first is that of the idealist, who lives in the world for his
ideals—a man of principles, intelligent, modest, moderate in
everything, patient, a man with manner, dreamy by nature, or a
deep thinker, a man of dignity who guards his reputation as one
would take care of a thin glass. His contact with the earth is like
that of a bird, who builds its nest upon a tree in the air, descends
to the earth to pick up a grain when hungry, then flies off. He
dwells on the earth because he is born on the earth, but in reality
he lives in his thoughts. The earth and all that belongs to the earth
is his need, not his want.

The second class is that of the artist—an artist not necessarily by
profession, but by nature. Artistic by temperament, this man shows
choice in his love; he is distinct in his likes and dislikes, subtle,
clever, witty, observing conventions and yet not bound by them;
one who notices everything and yet does not show himself fully;
elusive by nature yet tender and affectionate; fine and simple,
social and yet detached. He shows a likeness to a deer in the woods
who is one moment in one part of the forest and another moment
you will find him at quite a distance away. One may think by
coming into contact with him that one has got him, but at the next
moment one will find him far away from one's reach. This is the
type of man of whom many say, "I cannot understand him."

The third is the material man, material in his outlook, void of the love of beauty, concerned only with what he needs, clever but not wise. He lives all through life in the pursuit of earthly gains, ignorant of the beauty life can offer, looking from day to day with hope to that gain towards which he is working. In connection with this man one might say that he is waiting for the day when his ships will arrive.

The fourth is a man with mundane desires, who enjoys his food and drink. What he thinks about is his bodily comfort, his momentary pleasures, his passing joys—the slave of his passions and captive to the things of the earth. He is uninterested in everything but himself. He belongs to no one, nor does anyone in reality belong to him. He is happy-go-lucky by nature, yet susceptible to depression and despair. It is his case that one might say that he lives to eat.

These four different qualities belong to the body that the earth offers to the soul—the third and fourth classes more than the first and second. It is by this that one can trace back the origin of this clay that the soul has adorned and called it "myself"—this clay that has passed through so many different conditions while being kneaded; through the mineral, vegetable, and animal kingdoms it developed and then of it was made the image of man. "Verily in man is reflected all that is on the earth and in heaven."

The questions, why do souls come on earth, why has this creation taken place, what is the purpose of this manifestation, may be answered in one word: satisfaction—for the satisfaction of God. Why is God not satisfied without it? Because God is the only Being, and the desire of being is to become conscious of being. This consciousness experiences life through various channels, names, and forms, and in man this consciousness of being reaches its culmination. Plainly speaking, through man God experiences life at its highest perfection. If anyone asked, then, what is man's duty if that be the purpose, the answer is, his most sacred duty is to attain to that perfect consciousness which is his *dharma*, his true religion. In order to perform his duty he may have to struggle with himself, he may have to go through suffering and pain, he may have to pass many tests and trials. By making many sacrifices and practicing renunciation, he will attain that consciousness which is God-consciousness, in which resides all perfection. But why must man suffer and sacrifice for God? In the end of his suffering and sacrifice he will find that though he began to do so for God, in the end it has proved to be for himself. It is the foolishly selfish who is selfish, and the wisely selfish proves to be selfless.

Now comes the question, how may this consciousness be attained? It is to be attained by self-realization. First man must realize himself and find out of what he is composed. He is composed of spirit and matter. He consists in himself of the mineral, vegetable, and animal worlds, the genius and the angel, and it is his work to balance all this, knowing that he has neither been created to be as spiritual as an angel, nor to be as material as an animal; and when he strikes the happy medium he will certainly tread the path which is meant for a human being to tread, the path which leads straight to the goal. "Straight is the gate, and narrow is the way," narrow because any step taken on either side will lead to some path. Balance is the keynote of spiritual attainment. In order to attain to God-consciousness the first condition is to make God a reality, so that he is no longer an imagination.

No sooner is the God-ideal brought to life than the worshipper of God turns into Truth. There is no greater religion than Truth. Then Truth no longer is his seeking; then Truth becomes his being, and in the light of that absolute Truth he finds all knowledge. No question remains unanswered. That continual question that arises in the heart of man—"why?"—then becomes non-existent, for with the rising of every "why?" rises its answer. The moment a man has become the owner of the house, then he becomes acquainted with all there is in it; it is the stranger who finds it difficult to find any room in the house, not the one who lives in it; he knows about the whole house. What is rooted out in the quest of Truth is ignorance; it is entirely removed from the heart, and the outlook becomes wide, as wide as the Eye of God. Therein is born the divine Spirit, the spirit which is called divinity.

Has the sphere of the genius as many worlds as there are planets in the universe? Yes, as many, and as different from one another as the planets in the universe are different, yet not so far apart as in the universe, not so much out of communication with each other. Is the heaven of the angels created on the same model? Yes, but is it on the model of the heaven of the angels that our universe has been molded, and also that of the genii? What is life there? What is it like? It is difficult to explain and difficult to put into words, but for an example one might see the difference in the life of the birds which can fly over seas and forests, over hills and dales, and feel in tune with nature, and express their joy in song. Then the deer in the woods, dwelling in the caves of the mountains, drinking water at the natural springs, moving about in the open spaces, looking at the horizon from morning till evening, the sun their time-keeper and the moon serving as their torch. And then imagine our lives, the lives of human beings in crowded cities, days in the factories, and nights indoors, away from God, away from nature, even away from self; a life fully absorbed in the struggle for existence, an ever-increasing struggle of which there is no end. There is the picture before us, for us to imagine what life the angels live in the highest heavens, what life the genii live in the middle heaven, and compare with their lives our life as human beings in the universe.

Are there suns? Are there moons in their worlds as we have in ours? Yes, this outer solar system is the reflection of the inner solar system. What difference is there between time, the conception of time such as we have, and the idea of time they have there? There is an incomparable difference. No words will give the exact idea of the comparison between time, but for the sake of convenience let us say that our year is the hour of the genii and the moment of the angels. Are there angels and genii of longer and shorter lives, as men on earth? Certainly there are, but there is no comparison between the time of their life and that of the human being. Are there differences between the genii and the angels as among men of different sorts? Indeed there are, but among the genii not so many as among men, still less among the angels. What about the time that every soul spends in the heavens of the angels and the sphere of the genii? The speed of every soul is different. It is according to the speed with which they manifest; it is a different dimension. The difference of speed is like travelling on the earth, sailing on the water, and flying through the air. Difference of speed between different souls may be likened to one child advancing in its thought so that it may learn in ten years something which another could not learn in one hundred years of life on the earth. Nevertheless, as they say, "slow and sure." Souls with balance and rhythm throughout their manifestation learn and experience much more than by a rapid run through the heavens.

The word *akasha* in the language of the Hindus is expressive of a meaning that explains its object. *Akasha* means accommodation; not necessarily what man calls the sky, although the sky is an accommodation. On the model of the *akasha* the whole creation has been based. The organs of the senses—the ears, the eyes, the nostrils, the mouth—all are different aspects of *akasha*, and so is the human body constructed. The purpose of this construction can be found in its own nature; as the purpose of the ears is found in hearing, of the nostrils in breathing, of the eye in seeing, so is the purpose of the whole body. The purpose of the body is to experience life fully. For the intelligence the body becomes a vehicle by which it is able to experience life fully. In order to make sound more audible people build domes and other places, where this resonance is produced and the voice and the words become more clear. So the construction of the body is made to make all that is perceptible clear. By nature the body is the vehicle of the intelligence or the soul, by which it experiences life fully. But as man has lived for generations an increasing life of artificiality, he has moved farther and farther from nature; therefore this vehicle which was made a perfect instrument to experience life fully has become more and more incapable of attaining that object. It is this incapability of experiencing life fully and the innate desire to experience it, which makes the soul strive for spiritual attainment. What man does not know he thinks does not exist; in this is to be found the reason of materialism. But the tendency towards spiritual realization remains there as an innate desire which is consciously or unconsciously felt by every soul, whether spiritual or material. It is therefore that a material person has a silent craving in his heart to probe the depth of the spiritual ideal which he disowns.

The work of the senses is to experience, to taste, smell, touch, hear, and see; but besides these senses the inner sense is one sense. It is by experiencing through different organs of the senses that the one sense becomes many senses. It is the same sense that hears, smells, tastes, feels, touches; but because it experiences life through different organs, man divides one sense into five senses. The depth of that sense which is the inner sense is more subtle than a person can imagine. When that sense finds a free expression, it does not only experience life more keenly by the organs of the senses, but it becomes independent of the organs of sense. It penetrates through life deeply, and, as Kabir says: "It sees without eyes and hears without ears." The reason is this: that all that exists is contained in an accommodation, in the *akasha*, and by being in *akasha* the nature of all things is revealed. Plainly speaking, there is nothing in this world which does not speak. Everything and every being is continually calling out its nature, its character, and its secret; and the more the inner sense is open, the more it becomes capable of hearing the voice of all things.

In every person this sense exists, for the greater part hidden, buried; and its being buried gives discomfort, for it is something which is living—the only living being there is. The idea of the "Lost Word" has its secret in this; when once this inner sense has broken the walls around it, which keep it closed, it breathes the freedom and happiness which is the soul's own property; the soul attains. Every discomfort, from whatever source it comes, comes through the lack of understanding. The more the inner sense is covered, the more the soul finds itself in obscurity. It is therefore that the sign of the enlightened soul is readiness to understand. Therefore these souls are easy to reconcile. When a person can understand himself better, he can make another person understand better also. But when a person is perplexed himself he, instead of making another person understand, confuses him. In this way differences are produced.

The organs of the senses are the *akasha*s or accommodations of grosser and finer nature. The finer the organ the more perception it has; the grossness takes away from the organ its power of perception. This shows that the body may be likened to a glass house made of mirrors. In the Persian language the poets have called it *aina khama*, meaning the "temple of mirrors." The eye stands as a mirror before all that is visible; it reflects all that it sees. The ears are the accommodation for the re-echo of every sound that falls upon them. The senses of touch and of taste are grosser in comparison to the senses of sight and hearing. At the same time their nature is the same; all the different sweet, sour, and salt savours, and the feeling of warmth and cold, are perceived by them, and they stand as mirrors in which objects are reflected. Therefore, as in the mirror one sees oneself reflected, so this body stands as a mirror in which every experience of the outer life is reflected and is made clear. If the mirror is dusty it does not show the image reflected clearly, so the experience of life is not clear when the body is not looked after according to the spiritual point of view.

The Scriptures say that the body is the temple of God; but the right interpretation of this saying would be that the body is made to be the temple of God; a temple cannot be called a temple of God if God is not brought and placed there. So it is natural when a soul feels depressed that there is something wrong with the vehicle. When the writer wishes to work, and the pen is not in order, it annoys him; there is nothing the matter with the writer; it is the pen which is not right. No discomfort comes from the soul; the soul is happy by nature; the soul is happiness itself. It becomes unhappy when something is the matter with its vehicle, which is its instrument, its tool, with which to experience life. Care of the body, therefore, is the first and the most important principle of religion. Piety without this thought is of little significance. The soul manifests in this world in order that it may experience the different phases of manifestation, and yet may not lose its way and be lost, but may attain to its original freedom, in addition to the experience and knowledge it has gained in this world. The different exercises that the Sufis and Yogis do in

order to enable the mind and body to experience life more fully
—exercises such as fasting, pose, posture, movement—all these
things help to train the body, that it may become a fitting vehicle
for the experience of life. Wonder-working, such as psychometry,
feeling the atmosphere of places, of objects, of people—all this
comes when the body is also prepared for it. A person may be
intelligent, clever, learned, good, or pious, and yet his sense of
perception may not be fully awake. It must be remembered as
the first principle of life that manifestation was destined for
keener observation of life within and without.

The greatest unhappiness that a person feels is from lack of
mastery; the unhappiness comes when, knowing mastery, he yet
cannot practice that which he knows. Sadness comes from
limitation, limitation in different forms: lack of perception, lack
of power upon oneself or upon conditions, or from the lack of that
substance which is happiness itself—which is love. There is lack of
understanding, though there may be love; lack of love through
lack of understanding; there may be both things and lack of power.

If love has reached perfection it will attain all three powers;
when love becomes power, it becomes understanding. The nature
of love is as the nature of water in the depth of the earth. If one
does not dig deep enough one finds sand, not water, but when
one digs deep enough he finds water. Many lovers of God lose
patience, trust, and hope; they have touched sand and not reached
water, but when they have dug deep enough they find pure water.

As there are different organs of senses, so there are five
centers of inner perception. These centers denote seats of the
intuitive faculties. Two among these centers are of great
importance—the heart and the head. If the Sufi training differs
from that of the Yogis, it is in the training of both these centers
together, by which the Sufi produces balance. The head without
the heart shows dry intellect. The heart without the head

represents an unbalanced condition. Balance is the use of both these faculties. The Sufi training is based upon this principle. The centers may be likened to the space that one finds in the apple. It is an *akasha*—an accommodation—where not only scent, touch, hearing, and sight are perceived, but even the thought and feeling of another, the condition in the atmosphere, the pleasure and displeasure of one's fellow man are perceived; and if the sense of perception is keener, then even past, present and future are revealed.

When man does not perceive in this way it does not mean that it is foreign to his nature; it only means that the soul has not developed in his body that power of perception. The absence of such fine perception naturally causes depression and confusion, for the soul longs for a keen perception, and feels confused, and at times agitated, owing to a lack of a fuller perception, as the person who is blind feels nervous agitation, because the inner longing is to see, and when the organ of sight fails, he becomes agitated. This is the cause generally in many souls who feel restless. And when the life man lives is a life of artificiality, it works against him. It is not necessary to read the ancient traditions to find out the truth about this. Today in the people who live a less artificial life, a more simple life, a life in and near nature, the intuitive faculties are more keen, and they show a greater happiness. These centers become blocked by certain foods and by living a more materialistic life. These centers are located in certain places; and as there are some plants in the caves of the mountains where the sun does not reach and the air does not touch, and it is difficult for the plants to live; and so are the centers of perception located in the physical body; the body is nourished by food, but these centers remain without any nourishment. The physical body which is made of matter, its substance is matter; but the centers of perception are of still finer matter, and though they are located in the physical body, no nourishment can reach them, except that which is drawn through the breath, the fine substance which is not even visible. In the language of the mystics it is called *nur*, which means light.

The body does not only want food, but also breath—in other words, vibration—and that vibration is given to it by the repetition of sacred words. The sounds, the vowels, and the composition of the sacred words is chemical, and it is this process which was called by the ancient philosophers *chemi* or *alchemia*. These centers are the *akashas* or domes where every sound has its re-echo, and the re-echo once produced in this *akasha* or *asman* reaches all other *asmans* which exist within and without. Therefore the repetition of a sacred word has not only to do with oneself and one's life, but it spreads and rises higher than man can imagine, and wider than we can perceive. Verily every action sets in movement every atom of the universe.

When once the inner sense has become keen it shows its development first by working through the organs of the senses. The vision becomes clearer, the hearing becomes keener, the sense of touch felt more keenly, sense of taste and smell clearer. Therefore among those who tread the mystic path one finds many who are sensitive, and become more sensitive as they develop spiritually. As the standard of normal health known by the average person is much beneath the mystical ideal, often to the uninitiated the sensitiveness of a person of mystical temperament may seem peculiar. At the same time when it is developed by spiritual training, and this sensitiveness is under control, it manifests as the first thing in the life of a seer.

The body which covers the soul keeps it blind by depriving it of its freedom of expression in keener perception. It is like a captivity for the soul. When the centers of the body are awakened and at work, then the soul experiences life more clearly, and naturally clouds which give depression clear away. The soul begins to look forward to life with hope, with trust, and with courage; and thus attains that power and understanding which is needed in the struggle of life. When a little more advanced, the intelligence begins to see through the eyes what every eye cannot see—the finer forces of nature manifesting in color and form. There are many who talk much about this, and some who know and say little, for they do not see wisdom in speaking about something which the person standing next to them does not see. And among those who speak much about seeing things which others do not see, there is hardly one who really sees.

There is no doubt, as the sight becomes keen, first the colors of different elements working in nature manifest to the view; secondly, the atmosphere that is created around man, which is composed of semi-material atoms, becomes manifest to their eyes. This is what is called the *aura*. The different colors of the same denote the meaning, for there is nothing in this world which is without meaning. The one who pursues the meaning of life in all its aspects hears again in them the Word which was once lost for him.

No doubt the life of a sensitive person becomes difficult, especially when one has to live amongst the crowd. It is therefore for this reason the Brahmins lived an exclusive life, which has been criticized by some who do not know the meaning of it. Different practices of breathing become a great help in training both mind and body to make them more perceptive, in order that they may become fitting vehicles to fulfill the purpose of life.

The mind is made after the body. It is therefore that its form is that of the body. We read in the Old Testament that the heavens were made after the earth. The real place where the heavens are made is within man. The mind is made of all one learns, one experiences, one loves, and one remembers. It is therefore that man is that which his mind contains. If his mind contains a sorrow, man is sorrowful; if his mind contains joy, he is joyous; if it contains success, he is successful; if it contains failure, failure awaits him, everywhere he moves he finds failure. The mind is an accommodation in which man collects all that he learns and experiences in life. In short, man is his mind. How true, therefore, is the claim of the dervishes when sitting on the bare earth clad in rags; they address one another, "O king of kings, O monarch of monarchs!" That is their usual way of addressing one another. Their voice is the voice of true democracy, for this claim of theirs is the expression of their being conscious of the kingdom of God.

The mind is not only the treasure house of all one learns, but it is creative by nature. The mind improvises upon what it learns, and creates not only in imagination, but it finishes its task when the imagination becomes materialized. The heavens and the infernal regions are both the creations of the mind, and all are experienced in the mind. But the question is, is the body not born with a mind; did the mind not exist before the body? Yes, it did exist; it existed as an *akasha* or accommodation. And the question is, was this accommodation formed on any certain model or design? The first design of this *akasha* is molded upon the impression that falls deeply upon the soul, the soul coming towards manifestation from the infinite Spirit. If we picture the infinite Spirit as the sun, the soul is as its ray. The nature of the soul is to gather on its way all that it can gather, and all that it happens to gather, and make a mold out of it.

It is this impression that has helped the first mold of the mind to be formed. It manifests its original nature and character through the body with which it is connected and identified. The impression of the nature and character of the parents, of the ancestry, of the nation and race, follows after the first impression that the soul has taken on its way. If it happens to be the impression of one personality falling upon the mind going towards manifestation, in the life of that person the distinct characteristics of a certain personality who has lived in the past will show clearly. It is in this that the secret of the doctrine of reincarnation which the Hindus have held can be recognized. There are souls that come from the infinite to the finite existence, and there are spirits who return from the finite existence to the infinite, and their meeting ground is on the way. It may be one impression or it may be several impressions which help to mold this *akasha*, which, after it is once connected with the body, becomes the mind, for the mind is not complete until it is filled with the knowledge and experience the soul gains by the help of the physical body.

The mind is not necessarily the brain. The mind is a capacity, an *akasha*, which contains all the experiences we have in life; it has all the impressions we gain through our five senses. It is not only within the body but also around the body. But the centers of perception reflect every thought and feeling, and then man feels that the mind is within him. In point of fact the body is within the mind, and the mind within the body. As the eye sees an object before it, so the centers of perception reflect every thought and feeling. For instance, the sensation of joy and depression man feels in the center called *solar plexus*, but it does not mean that joy or depression is there, but that this center is sensitive to such experiences.

The mind for the sake of convenience may be called a substance, which is not physical matter, but a substance quite different from matter in its nature and character. There are some objects which give more resonance to sound, and there are other objects which respond less to sound. There are sonorous objects, such as metals of different kinds, which reproduce sound clearly, and then there are stones and solid wood which do not respond to sound. Such is the difference between mind and body. The mind is a much better vehicle for the intelligence than the body. Therefore, though the mind experiences life even through the material organs of the senses, still it itself is more perceptive and can experience life in its different aspects standing apart from the body. In other words, the mind can see for itself, it can even hear without the ears, for the mind has its own eyes and ears. Though it needs the physical eyes and ears to see and to hear, still there are things which the physical eyes and ears cannot see and hear. The mind sees and hears these. The more independent the mind is made of the outer senses, the more freely the mind perceives life and becomes capable of using the outer organs of senses to their best advantage.

To the question, has the mind a form, it may be answered that the mind has the same form as that with which the soul is most impressed. The question, what is the form with which the soul is most impressed, may be answered with: one's own. That is why, when man says "I," he identifies himself with the form which is most impressed upon his mind, and that is his own. But the mind is a world within itself—a magic world—a world which can be very easily changed, very quickly altered, compared with the physical one. The phenomenon of the mind is great, and wonders could be performed, if only one had the key of the mind in one's hand. The difficulty is that man becomes so fixed in his physical body that he hardly realizes in his life that he has a mind. What man knows of himself is of the body, though the mind; verily man is his own mind.

The mind is not only the *akasha*, which contains all that one learns and experiences through life, but among five different aspects of the mind, each having its own work, there may be one aspect which may be especially called the mind and which shows the power of the Creator. All that we see before our eyes, and all objects made by the skill of man, every condition brought about in life, whether favorable or unfavorable, are all the creation of the human mind—of one mind or of many minds. Man's failures in life, together with the impression of limitation which he has, keep him ignorant of that great power which is hidden in the mind. Man's life is the phenomenon of his mind; man's happiness and success, his sorrows and failures, are mostly brought about by his own mind, of which he knows so little. If this secret had been known by all, no person in this world would have been unhappy, no soul would have had failure. For unhappiness and failure both are unnatural; the natural is what man desires; the only question is, how to get it? The words of Emerson support this argument: "Beware of what you want, for you will get it." The whole life is one continual learning, and for the one who really learns from life, the knowledge is never enough. The more he learns, the more there is to learn. The secret of this idea is in the Koran: " 'Be!' He said; and it became." The seers and knowers of life do not only know this in theory, but by their life's own experience.

The mind has the power of creating; it creates all; but out of what does it create? Out of mazing *maya*, a substance subject to change, to death and destruction. However, the power of the mind is beyond question, and it teaches us that mostly our un-happinesses and failures are caused by our own mind more than by the mind of another, and if caused by the mind of another, our mind then is not in working order. The knowledge of the power of mind is, then, worth knowing when the moral conception of life is understood better, when man knows what is right and what is wrong, what is good and what is evil, and judges himself only, and sees these two opposite things in his own life, person, and charac-ter, for when man sees the folly of another, and wishes to judge another, then his sense of justice is not awake. The great ones whose personalities have brought comfort and healing to their fellow men were those who only used the faculty of justice to judge themselves, who tried to correct themselves of their own follies, and, being engaged in correcting themselves, had hardly time in life to judge another. The teaching of Christ: "Judge not, lest ye be judged," will always prove the greatest example to be followed.

The mind is a magic shell, in which a design is made by the imagination, and the same imagination is materialized on the surface, and then the questions, why does not all man thinks come true, why is not all he wishes realized, may be answered that by man's limitedness he, so to speak, buries the divine creative power in his mind. Life confuses man so much that there is hardly among a thousand one person who really knows what he wants; and perhaps among a million there is one who knows why he wants it; and even among millions you will not find one with the knowledge why should he want it, and why should he not want it. With all the power of the mind, one thing must be remembered: that man proposes, and God disposes. This will always prove true when man stands against the Will of God Almighty. Therefore the path of the saints in life has been to seek with resignation the Will of God, and in this way to swim with that great tide, that with the accomplishment of their wish the purpose of God may be fulfilled.

The key to the mind is the knowledge of life. There is only one real key; it is learnt in one moment; but the nature of life is such that we forget. The key to the mind is the knowledge of life; in other words, it is the psychology of life, and there is rarely a person who knows the psychology of life profoundly. Man has the faculty for knowing, but he is so absorbed in life that he does not give time to practice the psychology of life, which is more precious than anything in the world.

By psychology is meant that before uttering a word a man would think what effect it would have on the atmosphere, upon the person, on the whole of life. Every word is a materialization of thought; it has a dynamic power. If one considered, one would find that every little thought, every little feeling, every movement one makes, even a smile or a frown, such a small thing, if one knew the effect of every cause before bringing that cause into thought, speech, or action, one would become wise. Generally man does all mechanically, influenced by the conditions of the time, by anger or depression; so every man in life lives a life without control; in other words, without mastery. What we gain in spiritual knowledge is to gain mastery, to learn what consequences our actions will bring. A man cannot be perfect in this knowledge; all souls have their limitations; but it is something to strive after; in this is the fulfillment of God's purpose.

Even with this knowledge, knowledge alone does not make man capable; practice is necessary; and practice perhaps takes a whole life. Every day man seems to make more mistakes; this is not really so, but his sight becomes more keen. But what of those who do not think of all this? Every change of mood or emotion changes their actions, words, and thoughts, and so they can never accomplish the thing they have come to accomplish; all their life is passed in failure and mistakes, and in the end they have gained what they have made. So it is always true that life is an opportunity; every moment of life is valuable! To be able to handle oneself—if one has done this, one has accomplished a great deal.

The mind has different aspects, which are distinguished as the different departments which have their own work to do. First, the heart which feels, and which contains in itself four other aspects of mind; second, the mind which creates thought and imagination; third, memory; fourth, the will which holds the thought; fifth, the ego—that conception of mind which claims to be "I." There is no mind without a body, for the body is a vehicle of the mind; also it is made by the mind—not by the same mind, but by other minds. The child does not only inherit the form and feature of his parents and ancestors, but their nature and character; in other words, their mind which molds its mind and body.

The mind is not only the creator of thought, but it is the receptacle of all that falls upon it. The awakened mind makes the body sensitive to every different feeling. The sleeping mind makes the body dull. At the same time the fineness of the body has its influence in making the mind finer, and the denseness of the body makes the mind dense. Therefore the mind and body act and react upon one another. When there is harmony between the mind and body, health is secure and affairs will come right. It is the disharmony between mind and body which most often causes sickness and makes affairs go wrong. When the body goes south and the mind north, then the soul is pulled asunder, and there is no happiness. The secret of mysticism, therefore, is to feel, think, speak, and act at the same time, for then all that is said, or felt, or done, becomes perfect.

The different minds in the world may be likened to various mirrors, capable of projecting reflections and subject to reflect all that falls upon them. No one, however great in wisdom and power, can claim to be free from influences. It is like the mirror claiming, "I do not reflect all that falls upon me." Only the difference between the wise and foolish is that the wise man turns his back to what he must not reflect; the foolish does not only reflect the undesirable thought, but most proudly owns to it. The mind is creative and the mind is destructive; it has both powers. No thought ever born of the mind, be it even for a second, is lost.

Thought has its birth and death as has a living being, and the life of the thought is incomparably longer than that of any living being in the physical body. It is therefore that man is not only responsible for his action, but also for his thought. Souls would become frightened if they had a glimpse of the record of the thoughts they have created without meaning to create, under the spell of their ever-changing moods. As the Prophet has said, this life of the world which once was so attractive will one day appear before them as a horrible witch; they will fly from it, and will cry, "Peace, peace." It would not be an exaggeration if one called the mind a world; it is the world that man makes, in which he will make his life in the hereafter, as a spider weaves his web to live in. Once a person thinks of this problem he begins to see the value of the spiritual path. The path in which the soul is trained is not to be owned by the mind, but to own it; not to become a slave of the mind, but to master it.

It has been asked of the sages and thinkers of all times by the seekers after Truth that they should explain the meaning of the word *soul*. Some have tried to explain it, and some have given answers which are difficult for everyone to understand. In the meaning of the word *soul* many statements of thinkers differ, although all mystics arrive at the same understanding of the idea of the soul. As the air, by being caught in the water, becomes a bubble for the moment, and as the waves of the air, being caught in a hollow vessel, become a sound, so Intelligence, being caught by the mind and body, becomes the soul. It is only a condition of the Intelligence which is the soul. The Intelligence in its original aspect is the essence of life, the Spirit, or God. But when this Intelligence is caught in an accommodation such as body and mind, its original nature of knowing then knows, and that knowing Intelligence becomes consciousness. The difference between consciousness and the soul is that the soul is like a mirror, and the consciousness is a mirror which shows a reflection in it.

The Persian word *ruh* and the Sanskrit word *atma* mean the same thing: soul. There is another word, "sole" in the English language, which means one or single; although different in spelling, yet it is expressive of the same idea, namely, that the soul is that part of our being in which we realize ourselves to be one single being. When one thinks of the body, it has many organs; when one thinks of the mind, it has various thoughts; when one thinks of the heart, it has many feelings; but when one thinks of the soul in the right sense of the word, it is one single being; it is above division, and therefore it is the soul which really can be called the individual. Very often philosophers have used this name for the body, mind, and consciousness, for all three.

Sufism originally comes from the word *saf*, which means purity. This purity is attained by purifying the soul from all foreign attributes that it has acquired, thereby discovering its real nature and character. Pure water means something which is in its original element; if it happens that there is sugar and milk in the water, then the one who wishes to analyze it will separate the elements, and will try to see the water in its pure condition. Sufism, therefore, is the analyzing of the self, the self which has for the moment become a mixture of three things, of body, mind, and soul. By separating the outer garments of the soul the Sufi discovers the real nature and character of the soul, and in this discovery lies the secret of the whole life.

Rumi has said in the Masnavi that life on earth is a captivity of the soul. When one looks at the bubble in which the air has been caught by the water, one sees the meaning of Rumi's words, that something which is free to move about becomes captive by the atoms of water for a time, and loses its freedom for that moment. Man in all conditions of life, whatever be his rank, position, or possessions, has trouble, pains, and difficulties. Where do these come from? From his limitations; but if limitations were natural, why should he not be contented with his troubles? Because limitation is not natural to the soul, the soul who is by nature free, feels uncomfortable in the life of limitation. In spite of all that this world can offer, when the soul experiences the highest degree of pain it refuses everything in order to fly from the spheres of the earth and seek the spheres of liberty and that freedom which is the soul's predisposition. There is a longing hidden beneath all the other longings which man has, and that longing is for freedom. This longing is sometimes satisfied by walking in the solitude, in the woods, when one is left alone for a time, when one is fast asleep, when even dreams do not trouble him, and when one is in meditation, in which for a moment the activities of body and mind both are suspended. Therefore the sages have preferred solitude and have always shown love for nature, and they have adopted meditation as the method of attaining that goal which is the freedom of the soul.

The *Zat*, the primal Intelligence, becomes captive in knowledge; that which is its sustenance limits it, reduces it; and pain and pleasure, birth and death, are experienced by the Intelligence in this capacity which we call life. Death, in point of fact, does not belong to the soul, and so it does not belong to the person. Death comes to what the person knows, not to the person. Life lives, death dies. But the mind which has not probed the depths of the secret of life becomes perplexed and unhappy over the idea of death. A person once went to a Sufi and asked him what happened after death. He said: "Ask this question of someone who will die, of some mortal being, which I am not."

Intelligence is not only a knowing faculty, but creative at the same time. The whole of manifestation is the creation of the Intelligence. Time and space both are nothing but the knowledge of the Intelligence. The Intelligence confined to this knowledge becomes limited, but when it is free from all knowledge, then it experiences its own essence, its own being. It is this, which the Sufi calls the process of unlearning, which purifies and makes the Intelligence free from knowledge. It is the glimpses of this experience which are called ecstasy, for then the Intelligence has an independent joy which is true happiness. The soul's happiness is in itself; nothing can make the soul fully happy but self-realization.

Phenomena which the Intelligence creates by its creative power become as the source of its own delusion; as the spider is caught in its own web, so the soul is imprisoned in all it has created. This picture we see in the lives of individuals and of the multitude. Motive gives power, and at the same time it is motive which limits power, for the power of the soul is greater than any motive. But it is the consciousness of the motive which stimulates the power, and yet robs it of its power. The Hindus have called the whole phenomenon of life by the name *maya*, which means illusion, and once the true nature and character of this puzzle is realized the meaning of every word of language becomes untrue, except one Truth, which words cannot explain. Therefore the soul may be considered to be a condition of God, a condition which makes the only Being limited for a time; and the experience gained in this time, with its ever-changing joy and pain, is interesting, and the fuller the experience the wider becomes the vision of life. And what one has to experience in life is its true being. The life which everyone knows is this momentary period of the soul's captivity. Beyond this he knows nothing; therefore, every seeming change that takes place he calls death or decay. Once the soul has risen above this illusive phase of life, by climbing on to the top of all that is, besides itself, it experiences in the end that happiness for which this whole creation took place. The uncovering of the soul is the discovering of God.

The word *intelligence* as it is known by us and spoken in everyday language does not give a full idea; especially the word intelligence as used by modern science will only convey to us something which is the outcome of matter or energy. But according to the mystic, Intelligence is the primal element, or the cause as well as the effect. While science acknowledges it as the effect, the mystic sees in it the cause. One will question, how can the Intelligence create this dense earth, which is matter? there must be energy behind it. But this question comes because we separate Intelligence from energy or matter. In point of fact, it is spirit which is matter, and matter which is spirit; the denseness of spirit is matter, and the fineness of matter is spirit. Intelligence becomes intelligible by turning into denseness. That denseness being manifest to its own view, creates two objects: *Zat*, the Self, and *Sifat*, what is known by the Self. And then comes of necessity a third object, the medium by which the Self knows what it knows, *Nazar*, the sight or the mind. The Sufi poets have pictured these three in their verse as *Baak, Bahar,* and *Bulbul,* the garden, the spring, and the nightingale. And it is these three aspects of life which are at the root of the idea of trinity. The moment these three are realized as one, life's purpose is fulfilled.

As matter evolves so it shows intelligence, and when one studies the growing evolution of the natural world one will find that at each step of evolution the natural world has shown itself to be more intelligent, reaching its height in the human race. But this is only the predisposition of what we call matter which is manifested in the end; and everything in nature, even in the vegetable world, when we see it, is the seed of which the root is the evidence, and then the Intelligence, which is the effect, is also the cause.

Towards the Goal

The soul during its journey towards manifestation, and during its stay in any plane, whether in the heaven of the angels, the sphere of the genii, or the plane of human beings, feels attraction towards its source and goal. Some souls feel more attraction than others, but there is a conscious or unconscious drawing within felt by every soul. It is the ignorant soul, ignorant to its source and goal, who fears leaving the spheres to which it has become attached. It is the soul who knows not what is beyond who is afraid to be lifted up above the ground its feet are touching. Is the fish afraid of going to the depth of the sea? But, apart from fish, even men who are born on land and have been brought up upon the land, make a practice of swimming and diving deep into the sea and bringing up from the depths the pearl shells. There are seamen who are happier on the sea than on the land; and their daring, to those unaccustomed to the phenomenon of water, is sometimes perfectly amazing.

Life is interesting in its every phase, on the journey towards manifestation as well as on the soul's return toward the goal. Every moment of life has its peculiar experience, one better than the other, one more valuable than another. In short, life may be said to be full of interest. Sorrow is interesting as well as joy. There is beauty in every phase, if only one can learn to appreciate it. What dies? It is death that dies, not life. What, then, is the soul? The soul is life, it never touches death. Death is its illusion, its impression; death comes to something which it holds, not to itself. The soul becomes accustomed to identify itself with the body it adopts, with the environment which surrounds it, with the names by which it is known, by its rank and possessions, which are only the outward signs which belong to the world of illusion. The soul, absorbed in its child-like fancies in things that it values and to which it gives importance, and in the beings to which it attaches itself, blinds itself by the veils of its enthusiasm. Thus it covers its own truth with a thousand veils from its own eyes.

What is the return journey? Where does one return to? When does one return? The return begins from the time the flower has come to its full bloom, from the moment the plant has touched its summit, from the time the object, the purpose for which a soul is born upon earth is fulfilled, for then there is nothing more to hold it; and the soul naturally draws back as the breath is drawn in. But does man die by drawing in his breath? No. So the soul does not die owing to this drawing in, though apparently it gives to the dying person and to those who watch an impression of death. This physical body may be likened to a clock; it has its mechanism, and it requires winding, and this winding keeps it up. It is the healthiness of the physical body which enables it by its magnetic power to hold the soul which functions in it. As this body for some reason or other, either by disorder or by having been worn out, loses that power of keeping together by which it holds within, it gives way, and the soul naturally departs, leaving the material body as one would throw away a coat which one no longer needs.

The connection of the body and the soul is like man's attachment to his dress. It is man's duty to keep his dress in good order, for he needs it in order to live in the world. But it would be ignorance if he thought his dress to be himself, yet as a rule this is what man does. How few in this world stop to think on this subject—whether this body is myself, or whether *I am* apart from this body, higher or greater, more precious or longer living than this body. What, then, is mortality? There is no such thing as mortality, except the illusion, and the impression of that illusion, which man keeps before himself as fear during his lifetime, and as an impression after he has passed from this earth.

Both life and death are contrary aspects of one thing, and that is change. If there remains anything of death with the soul who has passed away from this earth, it is the impression of death, according to the idea it has had of death. If the soul has had a horror of death, it carries that horror with it. If it has agitation at the thought of death, it carries that feeling with it; also, the dying soul carries with it the impression of the idea and regard that those surrounding it in life had for death, especially at the time of its passing from the earth. This change for some time paralyzes every activity of the soul. The soul which has become impressed by the idea that it itself held of death, and by the impression which was created by those around the deathbed, keeps in a state of inertia which may be called fear, horror, depression, or disappointment. It takes some time for the soul to recover from this feeling of being stunned; it is this which may be called *purgatory*. Once the soul has recovered from this state it again begins to progress, advancing towards its goal on the tracks which it had laid before. How many souls are foolish in believing in the idea of death, and carrying with them that thought while passing from the earth to a life which is a still greater life? And how many souls do we find in the world who believe the end of life to be death—a belief in mortality which cannot be rooted out from their minds. The whole teaching of Jesus Christ has as its central theme the unfoldment towards the realization of immortality.

What is purgatory? Purgatory in the Sufic terms may be called *naza*, a suspension of activity. If there is any death it is stillness and inactivity. It is like a clock which for some time is stopped; it wants winding, and a little movement sets a clock going. So there comes the impulse of life, which, breaking through this cloud of mortality, makes the soul see the daylight after the darkness of the night. And what does the soul see in this bright daylight? It sees itself living as before, having the same name and form and yet progressing. The soul finds a greater freedom in this sphere, and less limitation that it has previously experienced in its life on the earth. Before the soul now is a world, a world not strange to it, but a world which it had made during its life on the earth. That which the soul had known as mind, that very mind is now to the soul a world; that which the soul while on earth called imagination is now before it a reality. If this world is artistic it is the art produced by the soul. If there is absence of beauty, that is also caused by the neglect of the soul of beauty while on earth. The picture of *jennat*, paradise, the ideas about heaven, and the conception of the infernal regions, is now to the soul an experience.

Is the soul sent to the one or the other place among many who are rejoicing there, or suffering for their sins? No, this is the kingdom that the soul has made while on earth, as some creatures build nests to stay in during the winter. It is the winter of the soul which is the immediate hereafter. It passes this winter in the world which it has made either agreeable or disagreeable for itself. But one might ask, does the soul live a solitary life in this world that it has made? No, how can it be solitary? The mind, the secret of which so few in the world know, this mind can be as large as the world, and larger still. This mind can contain all that exists in the world, and even all that the universe holds within itself. But one might say, what a wonderful phenomenon; I never thought that the mind could be so large; I thought my mind was even smaller than my body, that it was hidden somewhere in a corner of my brain. The understanding of mind, indeed, widens one's outlook on life. It first produces bewilderment, and then the vision of the nature of God, which is a phenomenon in itself, becomes revealed. Does one see, then, all those whom one has known while on the earth? Yes, especially those whom one has loved most, or hated most.

What will be the atmosphere of that world? It will be the re-echo of the same atmosphere which one has created in this. If one has learned while on earth to create joy and happiness for oneself and for others, in the other world that joy and happiness surrounds one; and if one has sown the seeds of poison while on earth the fruits of these one must reap there. That is where one sees justice as the nature of life. The idea of the prophets which one reads in the ancient Scriptures, that there will be a Judgment Day, and that man will be called before the great Judge to answer for his deeds, must not be understood literally. No, the Judgment Day is every day, and man knows it as his sight becomes more keen. Every hour, every moment in life, has its judgment, as the Prophet has said: "One will have to give account for every grain of corn one eats." There is no doubt about it, but why the Judgment Day has been especially mentioned in the Scriptures as taking place in the hereafter is because in the hereafter one cover has been lifted from the soul. Therefore the judgment which every soul experiences here on earth, and yet remains ignorant of, being unconscious of it, becomes more clearly manifest to the view of the soul after it has passed from this earth.

What connection has the soul which has passed from the earth with those who are still on the earth? No doubt there is a wall now which divides those on this earth from those in the other plane, yet the connection of the heart still keeps intact; and it remains unbroken as long as the link of sympathy is there. But why do the lovers of those who have passed away from the earth not know of the condition of their beloveds on the other side? They know it in their souls, but the veils of the illusion of the physical world cover their hearts, therefore they cannot get through clear reflections. Besides, it is not only the link of love and sympathy, but it is the belief in the hereafter to the extent of conviction in that belief which lifts those still on earth to know about their beloved ones who have passed over to the other side. Those who deny the hereafter deny to themselves that knowledge which is the essence of all learning. It is more easy for those who have passed from the earth to the other side to get into touch with those on the earth, for they have one veil less.

What does a soul do after having arrived at the sphere of the genius on its return journey? It continues to do the same things which it had been doing while on earth, right or wrong, good or evil. It goes along the same lines that it went on through life. Is there no progress for that soul? Yes, there is, but in the same direction. No ultimate change necessarily takes place; the soul finds itself in more clear spheres, therefore it knows its way better than it had done when on earth. What is its destination? The same destination. Though it may be hidden under a thousand objects, every soul is bound for the same goal. How can it be otherwise? Think how a person becomes attached to a place where he has been before, how one is attracted to a spot in a solitude where once one has sat and enjoyed the beauty of nature. How much, then, the soul must be attracted, either consciously or unconsciously, to its source, which is its eternal abode.

What connection do the souls who have passed from the earth have with those whom they have left on the earth? No particular connection, except that which is made by the link of love and sympathy. Do they all know of the conditions of the earth? If they care to. How can they know if they care to? Is there no wall between the people on the earth and those who have passed away? There is a wall which only stands before those who are still on the earth, but not before the ones who have passed over to the other side. They rise above this wall, so they see, if they care to see, the conditions of the world as clearly as we do, and even more so. Do they need some medium in order to observe the conditions on earth, or can they observe without any medium? No, they must have a medium, a medium on the earth, as their instrument, for they must have the physical eyes to see, the physical ears to hear, and the physical senses to experience life in the physical world. Then what do they do in order to experience life in the physical world? They seek for an accommodation in the heart of a being on the earth, and they focus themselves on the mind of that person, and receive through this medium all the knowledge and experience of this earth that they desire as clearly as the person himself. For instance, if a scientist wishes to learn something from the earth he may try to focus himself upon the mind of someone still in the body. He may choose an artist who knows nothing about science, and he can thus learn all he wishes about art, and yet the artist will remain as ignorant as before of science, except that he might have some vague idea of, or interest in, scientific discovery. Do the spirits always learn from the earth, or do they teach those on the earth? Both; they learn, and they also teach.

Are there any spirits who care little for the life they have left behind? Many, and among them good ones who are only con-cerned with the journey onwards. It is those as a rule whose heart is still attached to life on the earth, and in whose heart interest for the journey onward has not yet been kindled, it is they who are inclined to keep in communication with the earth. Yet there are exceptions. There are spirits who out of kindness to one, to a few, or to many, wish still to keep in connection with the earth in order to serve and to be useful. The spirits of this latter kind still go on advancing towards the goal instead of being detained when they communicate with the people on the earth.

What connection have the returning spirits with the inhabitants of the sphere of the genii? They are as far removed from them as one planet is from the other, yet being in the same universe. Do they meet with the inhabitants of that sphere? They do, but only such spirits as are not closed in or imprisoned or captive in their own world, those who have gained strength and power even while on earth to break the ropes that bind them and have liberated themselves from any situation, however difficult. But how do these brave ones arrive at this stage? By rising above themselves. If this limited self which makes the false ego is broken and one has risen above the limitations of life on all the planes of existence, the soul will break all boundaries and will experience that freedom which is the longing of every soul.

The soul which functions on its way to manifestation in different bodies covers itself thus with one body over another, which it uses to a smaller or greater degree in the renewing of the tissues of the body, or in healing it. The child born into a family in which there are physical infirmities is often born already healed from hereditary conditions and with its tissues renewed. The reason is because the soul is the divine Breath; it purifies, revivifies, and heals the instrument in which it functions. On its return journey the soul shows the same phenomenon in a different way, freed from all the impressions of illness and sadness and misery which it has experienced while on the earth and has taken into the spirit world; it heals its own being and renews the tissues of that body, which still remains with it after it has left the physical form. It purifies itself from all illness and the impression of illness, and thus renews the life in the spirit world in accordance to its grade of evolution. But, apart from evolution, it is the tendency of the soul to repel all that is foreign to it, either from the physical body or from the mental body, which it still has in the spirit world.

The soul is on a continual journey. On whatever plane it is, it is journeying all the time. And on this journey it has a purpose to accomplish—many purposes contained and hidden in one purpose.

There are objects which remain unfulfilled in one's lifetime on earth; they are accomplished in the further journey in the spirit world. For nothing that the human heart has once desired remains unfulfilled. If it is not fulfilled here, it is accomplished in the hereafter. The desire of the soul is the wish of God; small or great, right or wrong, it has a moment of fulfillment. If that moment does not come while the soul is on the earth plane, it comes to the soul in the spirit world.

The soul proves its divine origin on all the planes of existence, in creating for itself all it desires, in producing for itself the wish of its heart, in attracting and drawing to itself all that it wants. The source of the soul is perfect, and so is its goal; therefore, even through its limitation the soul has the spark of perfection. The nature of perfection is no want remaining. The limitation that the soul experiences is on the earth, where it lives the life of limitation. Still, its one desire is perfection, so every want is supplied, for the reason that the perfect One, even in the world of variety, does everything possible to experience perfection.

The soul coming to earth and its return—in both there is a process to be seen. When coming to earth it is adorning itself with the veils of the particular planes through which it passes, and on its return it unveils itself from the bodies it has adopted for its convenience in experiencing that particular plane. In this way there is a process of covering and uncovering. The soul, so to speak, throws off its garment on the same plane from which it borrowed it, when it has no more to do with it. Then what becomes of these bodies? Earthly bodies are composed of physical atoms, and so all that has been composed decomposes and returns to its own element; breath to air, heat to fire, liquid to water, and matter to earth.

In spite of all the diverse aspects in which the body may apparently be absorbed (various insects may eat it, birds may share it in their food, wild animals may devour it, or it may be swallowed by a fish, in time it may turn into the soil, or it may be used to nourish a plant or a tree), in every case the first rule remains. As the physical body composes and decomposes, so does the mental or spiritual body. This body has an incomparably longer life than the physical body has on the earth. Its end is similar to the end of the physical body. When the soul unveils itself of this mental garb it falls flat, as did the body of the earth, in that plane to which it belongs; for it is not the body which has strength to stand, the strength of standing belongs to the soul. It is therefore that man, in whom the soul manifests in the most pronounced form, stands upright, all other animals bowing or bending by their natural form.

Is the decomposing of the spirit body used in making the bodies there? Certainly it is, but not in such a crude way as happens with the earthly body; in a much finer way, for this is a finer body. There is joy in the composing or decomposing of this body, as there is even some pleasure in the composing and decomposing of the physical body. What does the body that the soul wears on the spirit plane look like? Ej actly the same as it looked on the earth. Why must it be so? Because of man's love for his body. Does this change? Yes, if it wishes to change; if the soul wishes it, it can be changed according to its own ideal. It can be made as young and as beautiful as possible; but it must be remembered that by nature the soul becomes so attached to its form that it clings to it, and as a rule it does not like to become different.

The condition of the next world is most like the condition of the dream world. In dreams one does not see oneself very different to what one appears, except in some cases, and at some times, and for that there are reasons. Nevertheless, the power that the soul has in the next world is much greater than that which it has in this world of limitations. The soul in the other world, so to speak, matures and finds within itself the power of which it was ignorant through life, the power of creating and producing all that it wished; and, its movements being not so much hindered by time and space, it is capable of doing for itself and of accomplishing things which are difficult for the soul to do and accomplish on the earth plane.

A soul which has passed from the earth and is in the spirit world can still live on the earth in one way, and that way is by obsessing another soul. Very often people have wrongly explained this idea, when they have said that the spirit takes hold of a dead body and, entering into it, makes use of it. The body once dead is dead; it has entered upon the process of returning to its own origin. It has lost that magnetism which attracts the soul and holds it, in order to allow it to function in the physical body. If the dead body had magnetism, then it would not have allowed the soul to return; it would have held it back, for it is the body which holds the soul to the earth; the soul has a pull from within which draws it continually towards its source.

But there are many living dead in the good or bad sense of the word. It is in these cases that a single-pointed spirit takes hold of their minds and bodies as its own instrument, using them to the best advantage; it is this which is generally known as obsession. In point of fact, there is no soul who has not experienced obsession in the true sense of the word, for there are moments in one's everyday life when those on the other side take the souls on the earth as their medium through which to experience life on the physical plane. Impression upon the soul is a much deeper experience than that which obsession gives, for in time the spirit who enters into the being of a person on earth makes that person entirely void of himself. He loses in time his identity, and becomes like the spirit who has obsessed him, not only in his thought, speech, and action, but also in his attitude and outlook, in his habits and manners, even in his looks, he becomes like the obsessing entity. Might one say, then, that it is a good thing from a mystical point of view to become thus selfless? No! this is not the way of becoming selfless; in this way one is robbed of the self. The mystical way of becoming selfless is to realize the Self by unveiling it from its numberless covers which make the false ego.

The soul on its return towards the goal in the sphere of the genii has collected during its life on the earth some riches in the form of merits, qualities, experiences, convictions, talents, and a certain outlook on life. In spite of the belongings of the earth which it has returned to the earth on its passing, these riches the soul in the spirit world offers or allows to be taken from it and imparts to the souls coming from their source who are on their way to the earth. These souls on their way to the earth, full of heavenly bliss but poor in earthly riches, purchase with the current coin of the plane of the genii, guarantees, contracts, mortgages, and all the accounts that the spirit had left unfinished on the earth; these they have to undertake to pay when coming on the earth. Among these souls who come there are some who take from one spirit all they can as their heritage from the spirit world. Some take from many; yet the souls who absorb, attract, conceive, and receive all that is given to them on the spirit plane have perhaps received more from one spirit than all the other gifts they have received from the various spirits they have met. Does this exchange rob the spirit on his way to the goal of his merits and qualities? No, not in the least. The riches that the soul can take to the sphere of the genius are safe and secure. Any knowledge or learning, merit or talent given to another person is not lost by the person who gives; it only makes the giver richer still.

When the Hindus said in the ancient times to a wicked person, "Next time you are born you will come as a dog or monkey," it was to tell him who did not know anything of life except himself, that his animal qualities would come again as the heritage of the animal world, so that he would not come again to the knowledge of his human friends, as a man, but as an animal. When they said, "Your good actions will bring you back as a better person," it was in the sense that the man who did not know the two extreme poles of his soul might understand that no good action could be lost, and for the man who had no hope in the hereafter and who only knew of life as lived on the earth, it was a consolation to know that all the good he had done would come again, and it was true in that sense of the theory which was thus explained.

It is only a difference of words. The soul who comes from above has no name or form, no particular identity. It makes no difference to the soul what it is called; since it has no name it might just as well adopt the name of the coat which was put on it, as that is the nature of life. The robe of justice put on a person makes him a judge, and the uniform of a policeman makes him a constable; but the judge was not born a judge, nor the constable a policeman; they were born on earth nameless, if not formless. Distinctions and differences belong to the lower world, not to the higher; therefore the Sufi does not argue against the idea of reincarnation. The difference is only in words; and it is necessary that a precaution be taken that the door may be kept open for souls who wish to enter the kingdom of God, that they may not feel bound by the dogma that they will have to be dragged back by their karma after having left the earth plane. The soul of man is the spark of God; though God is helpless on the earth, still He is all-powerful in heaven. And by teaching the prayer, "Thy kingdom come, Thy will be done on earth as it is in heaven," the master has given a key to every soul who repeats this prayer, a key to open that door wherein is the secret of that almighty power and perfect wisdom which raises the soul above all limitations.

Does the spirit impart its merits, talents, experiences, and knowledge consciously or unconsciously to the new-coming soul passing through the spirit spheres toward the earth? In some cases it imparts consciously, in others unconsciously. But in the conscious action there is the greatest pleasure for the spirit, for this soul, which is taking the knowledge from a spirit as its heritage from the sphere of the genius, is considered by the spirit as a child is by his parents or a pupil by his teacher. In giving the heritage to this soul there is a great joy for that spirit. Do they keep connection in any way? No connection except a sympathetic link, for one goes to the north and the other to the south; one ascending to heaven, the other descending to the earth. A connection or an attachment between them would do nothing but hinder the progress of both. A soul lives in the spirit world while it is busy accomplishing the purpose of its life, which may last for thousands of years.

Does a soul in the spirit world continue to do the same work which it did during its life on the earth? It does in the beginning, but it is not bound to the same work for this reason: that it is not subject to limitations as it was while on the earth. The soul eventually rises to that standard which was the standard of its ideal; it does that work which was its desire. Are there difficulties in the spirit world as on the earth in doing something and in accomplishing something? Certainly there are, but not so many as here on the earth. But what if there were one object that was desired by various spirits, how can they all attain to it? Will they all get some particles of that object? And if it be a living being, what then? The law of that world is different from the law of this world of limitations. There souls will find in abundance all which is scarcely to be found here on earth.

The picture of the spirit world is given in the story of Krishna. The gopis of Brindaban all requested the young Krishna to dance with them. Krishna smiled and answered each one that in the night of the full moon he would do so. All the gopis gathered in the valley of Brindaban, and a miracle happened. However many gopis there were, every gopi had a dance with Krishna, and all had their desire fulfilled, which is a symbolical way of teaching that the one divine Being may be found by every soul.

The spirit world is incomprehensible to the mind which is only acquainted with the laws of the physical world. An individual who is a limited being here is as a world there; a soul is a person here and a planet there. When one considers the helplessness of this plane one cannot for a single moment imagine the greatness, the facility, the convenience, the comfort, and the possibilities of the next world; and it is human nature that that which is unknown to man, means nothing to him. A pessimist came to Ali and said, "Is there really a hereafter for which you are preparing by telling us to refrain from things of our desire, and to live a life of goodness and piety? What if there be no such thing as a hereafter?" Ali answered, "If there is no such thing as a hereafter I shall be in the same situation as you are; and if there be a hereafter, then I shall be the gainer, and you will be the loser." Life lives and death dies; the one who lives will live, must live; there is no alternative.

Life in the sphere of the genius is the phenomenon of mind. The mind is not the same there, with all the thoughts and imaginations which it carries from the earth to this plane. Mind which is a mind here is the whole being there on the return journey; thoughts are imaginations here, but realities there. One thinks here, but the same action there, instead of a thought, becomes a deed, for action which here depends upon the physical body there is the act of mind. There is a picture of this idea in a story. A man who had heard of there being a tree of desire was once travelling and happened to find himself under the shade of a tree, which he felt to be restful and cooling, so he sat there leaning against it. He said to himself, "How beautiful is nature; how cooling is the shade of this tree and the breeze most exhilarating. But I wish I had a soft carpet to sit on and some cushions to lean against." No sooner had he thought about it than he saw himself sitting in the midst of soft cushions. "How wonderful," he thought, "to have got this." But now he thought, "If only I had a glass of cooling drink," and there came a fairy with a most delicious glass of cold drink. He enjoyed it, but said, "I would like a good dinner." No sooner had he thought of a dinner than a gold tray was brought to him, with beautifully arranged dishes of all sorts. Now he thought, "If only I had a chariot, that I might take a drive into the forest," and a four-horse chariot was already there, the coachman greeting him with bent head. He thought, "Everything I desire comes without any effort. I wonder if it is true, or all a dream." No sooner had he thought this than everything disappeared, and he found himself sitting on the same ground leaning against the tree.

This is the picture of the spirit world. It is the world of the optimist. The pessimist has no share in its great glory, for the reason that he refuses to accept the possibility which is the nature of life. Thereby he denies to himself all he desires and the possibility of achieving his desires. The pessimist stands against his own light and mars his own object here, and even more so in the hereafter, where the desire is the seed which is sown in the soil of the spirit world. Optimism is the water which rears the plant, but the Intelligence at the same time gives that sunshine which helps the plant to flourish on the earth as well as in the spheres of the genius.

Is there death for the spirits in the sphere of the genii? Yes, they have so-called death, but after a much longer time—a death not so severe as on the earthly plane, where everything is crude and coarse, but a change which is slightly felt after a very long life of the fulfillment of every desire. What causes this death? Are there illnesses or diseases? Yes, there are discomforts and pains peculiar to that sphere, not to be compared with the diseases in the plane of the earth. What especially brings about change in the sphere of the genius is the moment when hope gives way, and there is no ambition left. It is the loss of enthusiasm which is change there, and the cause of death here on the earth. Souls in the spirit world have more control over their life and death than those on the earth. The world of the spirit is his own world; it is a planet; when it loses that strength and imagination which holds the soul which is functioning in it, it falls like a star from heaven, and the soul departs to its own origin.

The soul now enters the angelic heavens, and it is allowed to enter under the same conditions as before. It has to leave all that belongs to the sphere of the genius in that sphere. Thus by unveiling itself of the garb of the spirit world, it finds its entrance into the world of the angels. Does it take anything to the world of the angels? Yes, but not thoughts; it takes the feelings that it has collected. The life of the soul, therefore, in this sphere is more felt by its vibrations. Every soul that enters the heaven of the angels vibrates in the same way to all that it has gathered during its life in the physical world and in the world of the genius. The example of this is manifest to our view here if we would observe life more keenly. Every person, before he does anything or says one word, begins to vibrate aloud what he is, what he has done, what he will do. There is an English saying, ''What you are speaks louder than what you say." The soul apart from the body and mind is a sound, a note, a tone, which is called in Sanskrit *sura*. If this note is inharmonious and has dissonant vibrations, it is called in the Sanskrit language *asura*, or out of tune. The soul, therefore, in the heaven of the angels has no sins or virtues to show; nor has it a heaven or hell to experience; nor does it show any particular ambition or desire.

It is either in tune or out of tune. If it is in tune it takes its place in the music of the heavens as a note in the tune; if it is not in tune it falls short of this, producing discordant effects for itself and for others.

What occupation has the soul there? Its occupation is to be around the light and life, like the bee around the flower. What is its sustenance? Its sustenance is divine light and divine love; divine beauty it sees, divine air it breathes, in the sphere of freedom it dwells, and the presence of God it enjoys. Life in the heaven of the angels is one continual music. Therefore it is that the wise of all ages have called music celestial, a divine art; the reason is that the heaven of the angels is all music; the activity, the repose, and the atmosphere there is all one symphony continually working towards greater and greater harmony.

What connection has the soul with the sphere of the genius once it has arrived in the angelic heavens? No connection necessarily, except a sympathetic link, if it happens to have such with anyone there, or if it happens that the body in which it functioned gives way before it has accomplished what it wanted to accomplish. The happiness of the angelic heavens is so great that the joy of the sphere of the genii cannot be compared with it and the pleasures of the earth are not even worth mentioning. For earthly pleasures are mere shadows of that joy which belongs to the heaven of the angels, and the joy of the sphere of the genius is like wine that has touched the lips but has never been drunk.

That wine one drinks on arriving at the heaven of the angels. In the Sufi terminology that bowl of wine is called *Jam-e Kauthir.*

There is a saying that there are four things which intoxicate the soul: physical energy, wealth, power, and harmony; but the intoxication that music gives excels all other forms of intoxication. Then imagine the music of the heavens where harmony is in its fullness; man here on earth cannot imagine the joy which that can give. If the experience of that music is known to anyone, it is to the awakened souls whose bodies are here, whose hearts are in the spheres of the genius, and whose souls are in the heaven of the angels; who, while on earth, can experience all the planes of existence. They call the music of the angelic spheres *Saut-e Sarmad* and find in it a happiness which carries them to the highest heavens, lifting them from worries and anxieties and from all the limitations of the plane of this earth.

What body has the soul in the heaven of the angels? The soul, though it continues in the sphere of the genius with a body of the likeness of that one it had while on earth, has undergone an enormous change which has taken place in its body and form while in the sphere of the genius, and when it reaches the angelic heavens there is still a greater change, for there it is turned into a luminous being. Its body is then of radiance; it is light itself. The only difference is that light as we understand it on the physical plane is of a different character; for it is here visible, but there it is both light and life in one; so the light is audible as well as visible, besides being intelligent. One may say that the physical body is intelligent also. It is; it is its intelligence which we call sensitiveness, but the body in the sphere of the genius is even more intelligent, and the body that remains in the angelic heavens is more intelligent still—it may be called Intelligence itself.

The life of the souls in the angelic heavens is incomparably longer than the life of those in the sphere of the genii. No more desires, no more ambitions, no more strivings have they; only aspiration to reach farther, to experience greater happiness, and to get closer to that Light which is now within their sight. They fly around this Light like the moth around the lantern; the "Magic Lantern," which is the seeking of all souls, is now within their horizon. Nothing has a greater attraction for them than this Light which is continually burning before them. They live and move and have their being in this divine Light.

Have they anything to offer to the souls going towards manifestation? Yes, their feelings. In what way do they offer them? Souls coming from the source and going towards the earth are tuned by them, are set to a certain rhythm. It is this offering which determines the path they tread in the future. The Sufis call that day of tuning *azal*, the day when the plan was first designed of the life of that particular soul. Does one soul only impress the soul newly coming towards earth with its tune and rhythm, with its feelings and sentiments? Not necessarily one soul; many souls may impress, but it is the one impression which is dominant. Is there any link or connection established between the souls who give and take one from the other? There is a link of sympathy, a feeling of love and friendliness, an impression of joy which a soul carries with it even to the destination to which it comes on the earth.

The crying of an infant is very often the expression of its longing for the angelic heavens; the smiles of an infant are a narrative of its memories of heaven and of the spheres above. Does the returning soul who meets with the new-coming soul receive anything? It does not require much; it is full of joy in its approach to the culmination of life, the goal of its journey. Yet the purity that the new-coming soul brings gives a new life and light and ease to the soul striving towards the goal, and illuminates its path.

The sizes of the bodies in the sphere of the genius and in the heaven of the angels are as numerous as on the earth plane. The size of the body that the soul brings from the sphere of the genius is much larger than the size of the physical body, and the size of the body brought by the soul from the angelic heavens is larger still. When the soul dons the body from the sphere of the genius, that body not only covers the physical body but also enters into it. And so the body brought from the angelic heavens covers both the body of the sphere of the genius and that of the physical plane, and yet enters into the innermost part of man's being. In this way the angelic and the genius bodies not only surround the physical body, but exist within it.

There is almost too much that a soul has to do on the earth; there is also much that it has to accomplish in the spirit world or plane of the genii. But there is much less to be done in the heaven of the angels; for as the soul proceeds forward, so its burden becomes lighter. The only condition of proceeding forward and drawing closer to the goal is that of throwing away the heavy burden which the soul has taken upon itself throughout its journey. If one may say that one soul lives in the spheres of the genii for thousands of years, for the sake of convenience one may use the expression "millions of years" in speaking of the time that the soul passes in the heavens of the angels; until at last there comes the moment when the soul is most willing to depart, even from that plane of love, harmony, and beauty, in order to embrace the source and goal of life, harmony, and beauty which has attracted it through all the planes. As the soul approaches nearer, so it has been drawn closer. It is the throwing off of that radiant garment which is its body in the angelic heavens that brings it to its real destination, the goal which it has continually sought either consciously or unconsciously.

What will be the mystery hidden behind the accomplishment of all desire in the next world to the earth plane? Will power, with optimism. It is the conviction which is called *yakeen* by the Sufis that will be the guiding light which will illuminate the path of the soul in the spiritual world. What will hinder the progress of the spirits is the lack of the same, though it is not necessary that the soul who has been pessimistic here must remain pessimistic in the next world. It is possible that its journey onward will bring about a change once the soul becomes acquainted with the mysteries of hopefulness.

In what way will the spirits communicate with one another? All spirits will not necessarily communicate; only those spirits who wish to communicate will do so. In what language? In their own language. If spirits did not know one another's language in the spirit world, there would not be such difficulty as on the earth, for there is one common language of that plane, a language which is the language of the spirit.

What is this journey taken by the soul from the source to manifestation, and from manifestation again to the same source which is the goal? Is it a journey, or is it not a journey? It is a journey in Truth. It is a change of experience, which makes it a journey, a story; and yet the whole journey produced in moving pictures is in one film which does not journey for miles and miles, as it appears to do on the screen. Do many journey or one? Many while still in illusion, and one when the Spirit has disillusioned itself. Who journeys, is it man or God? Both and yet one—the two ends of one line. What is the nature and character of this manifestation? It is an interesting dream. What is this illusion caused by? By cover upon cover; the soul is covered by a thousand veils. Do these covers give happiness to the soul? Not happiness, but intoxication. The farther the soul is removed from its source, the greater the intoxication. Does this intoxication help the purpose of the soul's journey towards its accomplishment? It does in a way, but the purpose of the soul is accomplished by its longing. And what does it long for? Sobriety. And how is that sobriety attained? By throwing away the covers which have covered the soul and thus divided it from its real source and goal.

What uncovers the soul from these veils of illusion? The change which is called death. This change is either forced upon the soul against its desire, which is then called death, and which is a most disagreeable experience like snatching away the bottle of wine from a drunken man, which is for the time most painful to him; or the change is brought about at will, and the soul throws away the cover that surrounds it, and attains the same experience of sobriety while on earth, even if it be but a glimpse of it; the same experience which, after millions and millions of years, the soul, drunken by illusion, arrives at, and yet not exactly the same. The experience of the former is *fana*, annihilation, but the realization of the latter is *baka*, the resurrection. The soul, drawn by the magnetic power of the divine Spirit, falls into it with a joy inexpressible in words, as a loving heart lays itself down in the arms of its beloved. The increasing of this joy is so great that nothing the soul has ever experienced in its life has made it so unconscious of the self as this joy does; but this unconsciousness of the self becomes in reality the true Self-consciousness. It is then that the soul realizes fully that "I exist."

But the soul which arrives at this stage of realization consciously has a different experience. The difference is like that of one person having been pulled with his back turned to the source, and another person having journeyed towards the goal, enjoying at every step each experience it has met with, or rejoicing at every moment of this journey in approaching nearer to the goal. What does this soul, conscious of its progress towards the goal, realize? It realizes at every veil it has thrown off a greater power, an increased inspiration, until it arrives at a stage, after having passed through the sphere of the genii and the heaven of the angels, when it realizes that error which it had known, and yet not known fully; the error it made in identifying itself with its reflection, with its shadow falling on these different planes.

It is as if the sun had thought by looking at the sunflower, "I am the sunflower," forgetting at that moment that the sunflower was only its footprint. Neither on the earth plane was man his own self, nor in the sphere of the genii, nor in the heaven of the angels. He was only a captive by his own illusion, caught in a frame; and yet he was not inside it, it was only his reflection. But he saw himself nowhere, so he could only identify himself with his various reflections, until now that the soul realizes it is *I* who was, if there were any. What I had thought myself to be was not myself, but was my experience. I am all that there is, and it is myself who will be, whoever there will be. It is I who am the source, the traveller, and the goal of this existence. Verily Truth is all the religion that there is, and it is Truth which will save.

The Phenomenon
of the Soul

The Philosophy of the Soul

The soul is called in Sanskrit *atma*, in Persian it is called *ruh*. When the Prophet was asked, "What is the soul?" he answered in two words, "*Umri Allah*" (an activity of God).

The connection between the consciousness and the soul is like the connection between the sun and the ray. The ray is formed by the activity of the sun shooting forth its light. The activity of the consciousness shoots forth its ray, which is called the soul. Activity in a certain part of the consciousness makes that part project itself toward the manifestation. The ray is the sun, but we distinguish the ray as apart, distinct with itself, longer or shorter, stronger or fading away, according to the state of activity in it.

The soul during its life on earth and after does not change its plane of existence; if any change takes place it is in the direction of its movement. The soul has originally no weight, but on its way it gathers around it properties produced from itself and borrowed continually from the elements which compose the universe. As our possessions are not necessarily ourselves, so the properties are not the soul. The best comparison is with our eyes, in which vast tracts of country, huge mountains and miles of horizon of the sea are reflected at one time, and yet the eyes are scarcely an inch in length and width. Such is the nature of the soul, which is so small as to be counted one among the numberless souls contained in the universe and yet so vast as to contain within itself the whole universe.

The external self, the mind, and the body have confined a portion of the whole consciousness; the same portion is in reality the soul. It is as if a line were drawn upon a cloth marking off a part of it as separate from the whole. Or it is as if we were to stand before a curtain with a small lantern so that the light of the lantern falls upon the curtain and forms a patch upon it. In like manner the impressions of the mind and body are reflected on the soul and separate it from the whole consciousness. Upon the soul is reflected the happiness or misery, the joy or sorrow of the external self, but the soul in itself is neither sad nor joyful. The soul is neither subject to birth and death nor has it increase or decrease; it neither evolves nor degenerates.

If you stand before a mirror clothed in rags the mirror holds the reflection of your rags, but it is not itself in misery. If you stand before the mirror covered with pearls and diamonds the reflection of your pearls and diamonds falls upon the mirror, but the mirror does not turn into diamonds or pearls. So it is with the soul; neither is it a sinner nor is it virtuous; neither is it rich nor is it poor. All life's joy and sorrow, rise and fall, are reflected for the time being upon the curtain of the soul, and after a time pass away. It is therefore that both the joy and sorrow of yesterday are nothing to us today.

The soul and the body are the same essence; the soul has formed the body from itself, the soul being finer, the body grosser. What in the soul may be called vibration, in the body becomes atom. The soul has become mind in order to experience more; it has become body in order to experience still more concretely. Yet the mind is independent of the body, and the soul is independent of both mind and body.

The soul sees through the mind and the body; the body is the spectacles of the mind, and the mind is the telescope of the soul. It is the soul that sees, but we attribute sight and hearing to the eyes and ears. In the absence of soul neither the body nor the mind can see. When a person is dead the eyes are there, but they cannot see; the ears are there, but they cannot hear.

It is the work of the soul to know and to see, and it is the work of the mind and body to act as a magnifying glass for it. Yet they in their turn also see and hear what is external to them, as the consciousness works through them also. The soul sees the play of thought in the mind; the mind perceives the pains and sensations of the body; the body is conscious of heat, cold, and touch. Its consciousness may be seen when something is accidentally about to fall on it. Before the mind can think of a plan for safety, the exposed part of the body instantly contrives its escape.

The mind sees the body alone, but the soul sees both the mind and the body; neither the body nor the mind is able to see the soul. The soul is accustomed to see what is before it, and so it cannot see itself. Our soul has always looked outward; that is why our eyes, nose, ears, all our organs of perception are outward. It is our mind and our body that attract our soul outward. And as the eyes, which see all things, yet need a mirror to see themselves, so the soul cannot see itself without a mirror.

When the eyes are closed, do you think that the soul sees nothing? It sees. When the ears are closed, do you think that the soul hears nothing? It hears. This proves that it is the soul that sees and hears. In the meditative life, by viewing the *anvar* and *ansar*, a Sufi realizes the fact that there are objects which, without the help of the eyes, the soul can see, and there are sounds which, without the help of the ears, it can hear. The great poet Kabir has said, "What a play it is that the blind reads the Koran, the deaf hears the Gita, the handless is industrious, the footless is dancing." He refers to the soul which has the capacity of working even without instruments, such as the organs of the body and the faculties of the mind.

Sleep, the unconscious condition, is the original state of life, from which all has come. "The world was created out of darkness" (Koran). As the body sleeps and the mind sleeps, so the soul sleeps. The soul does not always sleep at the same time as the mind and the body. This sleep of the soul is experienced only by the mystics; they are conscious of this experience in themselves and so can recognize it in others. The body sleeps more than the mind, the soul sleeps much less than either the mind or the body. When a person is fast asleep his soul does not lose its contact with the body. If the soul lost its contact with the body, the person would die; if the soul withdrew from the mind, the mind would be dispersed, the collection of thought would be scattered. It would be like a volcanic eruption.

The soul takes pleasure in the experience of the senses, in eating and drinking, in every experience. It indulges in this, and the more it indulges in it the more it becomes bound to this. All that we eat and drink contains a narcotic, even pure water. Therefore after eating and drinking a sort of sleep comes upon us. The soul feels a little relieved; it feels rather detached from the body. The soul cannot easily be free from the body and the mind. Though its real joy is to attain peace by being free from experience, yet it has forgotten this. "Happy is he who keeps it pure and lost is he who corrupts it" (Koran). There are people who take strong drink, hashish, opium, drugs, and all such things. Under their influence the troubles of the body are felt less, the thoughts are blurred, and the soul feels relieved; but it is a transitory happiness because it is dependent upon matter instead of upon spirit.

The ordinary person knows that after deep sleep he is calm, he feels reposed, his feeling is better, his thoughts clearer. The condition of *hal* or *samadhi*, the highest condition, is the same as that of deep sleep, the difference being only this, that it is experienced at will. The difference between the perfect person and the ordinary person is only this, that the perfect person experiences consciously what the imperfect person experiences unconsciously. Nature provides all with the same experience, but most people are unconscious of the experience, which is to their disadvantage.

When the mind is dispersed, no impression will remain on the soul, nothing will retain it from merging into the whole consciousness.

It has been said by some philosophers that we are parts of God. That is not so. They have said this because they have seen the physical body. What more can the intellect see? In the physical existence, each individual is distinct and separate, but behind this physical existence all are one, the consciousness is one. If it were not so we should not be able to know one another, neither the face nor the voice nor the language each of the other. We can know, if we advance spiritually, how our friend is. If he is in Japan or in Arabia and we are here, we can know if he is ill, or whether he is sad or happy. And not the state of our friends only, but everything is known to the advanced soul.

Manifestation

In the beginning, when there was no earth nor heaven, there was no other phase of existence than the eternal consciousness, which in other words may be called a silent, inactive state of life or unawakened intelligence that man has idealized as God, the only Being.

In the first stage of manifestation the unconscious state of existence turns into *'Ilm*, consciousness. Every soul is a ray of the consciousness. The nature of the consciousness is that it is radiant, it sends out rays. These pass through all the planes until they reach the ideal manifestation in man.

In the Vedanta the soul is called by three names which denote its three aspects, *Atma, Mahatma, Parmatma*. Atma is the soul conscious of the life on the surface; Mahatma is the soul conscious of the life within as well; Parmatma is the consciousness that is the soul of souls, conscious of the absolute within and without, the God of the knower, the Lord of the seer.

In the primal stage of manifestation the consciousness has no knowledge of anything save of being, not knowing in what or as what it lives. The next aspect of the consciousness is the opposite pole of its experience, where it knows all that is seen and perceived through the vehicles of the lower world, but is limited to this. When it rises above this experience and experiences the higher world as far as the highest aspect of its being, as said above, it becomes Mahatma, the Holy Ghost that unites Parmatma, the Father, with Atma, the Son, as explained in the terms of Christianity.

All this manifestation is constituted of two aspects of the consciousness, power and intelligence, in poetical terms love and light. All power lies in the unintelligent aspect of the consciousness, and the wisdom of the Creator that we see in the creation is the phenomenon of the intelligent aspect of the consciousness.

All this creation is not created of anything that is outside of the consciousness. It is the consciousness itself which has involved a part of itself in its creation while a part remains as Creator, as water frozen turns into ice and yet water abides within and the ice lasts only for the time that it is frozen; when light reaches the ice it turns into water, its original element. So it is with the consciousness; all things have been created out of it, and when their time of existence is finished all return and merge into it.

The consciousness has taken four distinct steps in manifestation which in the Sufic terms are called *'Ilm, 'Ishq, Ujud, Shudud. 'Ilm* is the stage in which the consciousness acts as intelligence. *'Ishq* is the stage when the activity of the rays of the consciousness has increased and this has caused confusion among the rays and made power out of the intelligence, which is will in a simple term and in a poetical term love. The third step of the consciousness is the creation of vehicles, such as mind and body, through which it experiences the life on the surface. And its fourth step is its conscious experience of life from the depth to its utmost height, which is called *Shudud*, and this fulfills the purpose of all manifestation.

The divisions of one into many are caused by light and shade, and if we looked keenly into life, both within and without, we should realize clearly that it is one life, one light, which appears divided and made into many by different shades. Every luminous object under the shadow of a less luminous object turns darker in part, and this in the term of art is called shade. It is this secret which is hidden under the variety of things and beings.

Time and space are the cause of all creation and the source of all its variety. It is time that changes things and beings from the raw state to the ripe condition, from youth to age, from birth to death. Time brings rise and fall, and space gives success and failure. A person may meet with failure in one place and in another place with success, in one country he may rise and in another country he may fall. If one were to look closely into life one would see that all creation is changed under the influence of time and space, whereas no change ever takes place in space or in time. It is in these that the mystery of the whole world abides.

The activity of the consciousness has two aspects, motion and stillness, which cause two distinct things, the expressive power and the faculty of response. From the highest to the lowest plane of existence and in the life of all things and beings we see these two forces working unceasingly, each being for the other, and in the experience of expression and response lies the joy of both, in other words, the satisfaction of the consciousness. The sun expresses, the moon responds; the voice expresses, the ear responds. All the dual aspect in life, such as male and female, shows these two aspects. There is not a single thought, speech, action, or event that takes place without the activity of these two, all happiness and success being in their harmony and every fall and failure in its lack. The birth of every thing and being is caused by the meeting of their glance, and death and destruction is the result of their conflict, when either merges into the other and both lose their power.

There are two different ways in which creation takes place from the highest to the lowest plane, intention and accident. The former shows the wisdom of the Creator, which creates all things suited to their purpose, and accident is that which shows in things and beings loss of purpose. All the opposites, such as good and evil, sin and virtue, right and wrong, beauty and ugliness, are accounted for by the above two tendencies of the Creator that work throughout the creation.

The whole creation acts under the law of attraction and repulsion, the former being the affinity which collects and groups atoms and vibrations and all things and beings, this being power and repulsion the lack of it. It is these two that uphold the universe; if one of them were to cease to exist the whole universe would crumble to pieces.

The life of the universe in all its workings is entirely dependent upon the law of tone and rhythm.

The pure consciousness has, so to speak, limited itself more and more by degrees by entering into the external vehicles, such as the mind and the body, in order to be conscious of something, for the joy of every thing is experienced when it is essayed.

The first state of manifestation of the consciousness is of a collective nature, in other words a universal spirit, not individual. There is a saying of a dervish, "God slept in the mineral kingdom, dreamed in the vegetable kingdom, awakened in the animal kingdom, and realized Himself in the human race." Therefore the ultimate aim of the eternal consciousness in undertaking a journey to the plane of mortality is to realize its eternal being.

Each of the said kingdoms has sprung from the preceding one and each preceding kingdom has developed into the succeeding kingdom. In the mineral kingdom one sees by a careful study how the rock has developed into metal, and from metal into softer earthy substance, until it develops into the plant. And one sees how the development of the plant creates germs and worms, which we call lives, and how from their germ and worm state of being they develop into insects, birds, and beasts. This all shows that nature is working continually to rise to a greater consciousness of life, and finds its satisfaction at last when it has accomplished its journey by rising, and has risen to its natural and normal state of being, which is accomplished in man.

The Law of Heredity

Heredity has been much thought of among all peoples and in all ages. If we look at the animal kingdom we see that the lion cub is never the offspring of the snake nor are toads hatched from pigeon's eggs, the oak tree will not produce dates nor do roses spring from thistles. We see in the East that of all breeds of horses the Arab horse is the best. One slight touch of the whip will make it leap any obstacle, cover any distance, while there are other horses that are like donkeys, on whose backs dozens of lashes are laid and they put one foot forward and stop, and again twenty lashes are given to them and they take one step forward. The Arabs value their horses so highly that they reserve the breed and never allow it to be mixed with any other strain. Among dogs there are some who will follow anyone. Whoever gives them a bone is their master, and if another person gives them meat, they leave the first and run after the other. And there are others who follow only one master, who obey only one and sometimes even sacrifice their life for him. It depends upon the breed, the heredity.

In the East they have considered this subject of heredity very much and have given great importance to it. We have always seen that the son of a poet will be a poet, the son of a musician is expected to be a musician. If a man handles weapons they ask him,

"Are you the son of a soldier?" The son of a miner will never do
the work of a shepherd, and the son of a shepherd will never do
the work of a miner. A great many of the words of abuse have
more to do with the parents than with the person to whom they
are addressed, and a great many words of praise have to do with
the ancestors, not with the person of whom they are spoken. In
India we have a family of poets who have been poets for ten or
fifteen generations. They are in Rajputana, and all of them are
great, wonderful poets. They are called *Shighrakavi*, improvisors,
and are appointed in the courts of the maharajahs. Their work
is to stand up upon any occasion in the assembly and, seeing the
occasion and the people present, to recite verses, in rhyme and
meter, in the manner suited to the occasion. In ancient times,
when sons of kings and great people were often driven from their
country and wandered unknown in other lands, the way of recog-
nizing them was always by some test of their quality. It has
happened in the history of the world that slaves have become
kings, and yet they could not keep themselves from showing
from the throne, through their grandeur, glimpses of their slavish
nature.

You may ask whether it is the soul that transmits its qualities, or
the mind that transmits its qualities, or the body? This is a vast
subject. Before explaining it I will say, as to the word *soul*, that
there are some people who call *soul* those qualities that compose
the individuality. This is not the soul but the mind. The soul has
no qualities, it is the pure consciousness and therefore it does not
transmit any.

When the soul first starts from its original point, it comes first
to the world of the *fereshta*, the angels, and is impressed with
the angelic qualities. The angels are absorbed in the hunger for
beauty and the thirst for song. They do not distinguish good and
bad, high and low. The infant, who represents the angel on earth,

always turns to what appears to it radiant and beautiful. There are two sorts of angels, those who have never manifested as man, and those spirits who upon their way back to the infinite have reached the world of the angels. Love, light, and lyric are the attributes of the latter; from them the soul receives these impressions. Devotion, service, and worship are the attributes of the former. The angels are masculine and feminine; the former are called *malak*, the latter *hur*.

In the world of the angels the soul for years and years enjoys these experiences. When the desire for more experience urges it on, it goes forth and comes to the world of *djinns*, which is the astral plane. In the Bible we read that Adam was driven out of paradise; this means that the wish for more experience makes the soul leave the world of the angels and go to the astral plane and the physical plane.

The occupation of the djinns is to imagine, reason, and think. The djinns are of two sorts: there are those who have never manifested physically and there are those spirits who have left the earth with all the load of their actions and experiences upon them. The djinns also are masculine and feminine, and are called *gulman* and *peri*.

The soul, on its journey from the unseen to the seen world, receives impressions from the souls which are on their return journey from the seen to the unseen. In this way the soul collects the first merits and qualities. It is this which forms a line for the soul to follow, and it is this line that leads it to the parents from whom it inherits its later attributes. The soul receives the impressions of another soul if it is attuned to that other soul. For instance, a soul meeting the soul of Beethoven receives the impression of Beethoven's music, and then is born with the musical qualities of Beethoven. The upholders of the theory of reincarnation say, "He is the reincarnation of Beethoven." The

Sufi says that if it is meant that Beethoven's mind is reincarnated in him, it may be said; but because the spirit is from the unlimited, he says it need not necessarily be called reincarnation. Therefore a person of poetical gifts may be born in the family of a statesman where there never before was a poet.

Each soul is like a ray of the sun or of any light. Its work is to project itself, to go forth as far as it can. It is creative and responsive. It creates its means, its expression. and it is impressed by whatever comes before it, in proportion to its interest in that. The soul goes always to what appears to it beautiful and radiant, and so it goes on and on and finds different qualities and different experiences and collects them around it, until at last it finds the mother's womb.

A child may either inherit the qualities and defects of its parents or it may not inherit them. If the impressions previously received by the soul are stronger it does not inherit them. Very wicked parents may have a very saintly child, and very good parents may have a very bad child.

The mental attributes of the parents are inherited by impression on the mental plane. The thought, the feeling of the parents are inherited by the child as a quality. If the father is engaged in thinking, "I should build an orphanage," the child will have a philanthropic disposition. If the father is thinking, "This person is my enemy, I should revenge myself on him," the child will have a vindictive disposition. If the mother admires something very much, if she thinks, "How beautiful these flowers are," the child will have that love of beauty in its nature. Also the qualities and features of the relations and other persons of whom either of the parents thinks most are impressed on the child.

You will ask me, "A child is often like an uncle or an aunt of the father or mother; why is this?" This has two aspects. It may be either that the father or mother has the qualities of this relation, although in them they have not fully developed, and those qualities develop in the child; or that the grandmother or grandfather or other relation has so much attachment for his descendants that his spirit watches and impresses with his qualities the child that is born in that family.

It is true that genius is transmitted by heredity and develops at every step, but it is sometimes found that the child of a very great person happens to be most ordinary; sometimes the child of a most worthy person proves to be most unworthy. This may be explained in the following manner: every manifestation of genius has three stages, *uruj*, *kemal*, and *zaval*, ascent, climax, and decline. When the genius is in the ascendant it develops more and more in every generation; when it reaches its climax it surpasses all previous manifestations of genius in that family; when it is in the decline it shows gradually or suddenly the lack or loss of genius. It is thus with families, nations, and races.

That which is more outward is given in heritage more than what is more inward. A man may not be very like his father in looks or nature, yet he inherits his property; the state will give the property to the son. It is inherited because it is more outward. The qualities of the body are inherited more than those of the mind, because they are more outward.

Every physical atom of the parents becomes radiant and its qualities are imparted to the child. In the case of a father who has liked drink, the child, of course, is born without the tendency for strong drink at the moment, but as it grows and develops, the cells of its body, being the same as those of the father's, may have the same craving for drink. And so it is with all vices; though the parents would never wish to impart them to their children, yet they do so unconsciously by their weakness and neglect.

Man has often so much concern for his posterity that he earns money and amasses it, not spending it for himself, in order that he may leave it to his children. He even gives his life on the battlefield that his children may enjoy the fruits of the victory. But if he only knew how much influence the life that he leads has on his posterity he would think it of more value to keep his life pure and elevated, both in health and mind, in order that his children may inherit the wealth of humanity, which is much more precious than earthly wealth and possessions.

Coming now to the question whether more qualities are inherited from the paternal side or the maternal side, I will say that the qualities inherited from the father are more deep-seated, while those inherited from the mother may be more apparent, because the father's inheritance is the substance, the mother's is the mold. The soul has many more attributes of the father because these are the fundamental, original attributes. The attributes of the mother are added to these; they are more active because they are later attributes. Those qualities which are first impressed upon the soul are stronger and those attributes which are acquired later are more active. From association with its mother, from her training, a child acquires very many of her attributes. A man may not like the qualities of his father and may hide them. A small child may have a face just like his mother's, but at some period of his life he will grow so like his father in looks that it is astonishing. A coward by association with brave people may become brave; he may go to the war, but then, when he bears the guns, the cowardice which was the original attribute of his soul will show itself. A child may be very like its mother in appearance, yet the quality is the father's. For instance, if the father is very generous, and the mother is finer, the child will, perhaps, be generous and finer. In this way the evolution of the world goes on by the intermingling of nations and races. Those families who keep themselves segregated in the end become weak and very stupid. For this reason the Prophet in Islam allowed all races and castes to intermarry, because the time had come for the human race to evolve in this way.

You will say, "Then, if we inherit the attributes of our father, our mother, our grandfather and forefathers, and acquire the attributes of the djinns and angels, how can we help how our character is?" A man may say, "I have a quick temper because my father had a quick temper, I have a changeable disposition because that is in my family; I cannot help this, it is my character." This is true in part, but it is developed by belief in it. The soul acquires and casts off attributes and qualities throughout life. A coward who joins the army by hearing always of bravery, by living with soldiers, may in time feel inclined to go to the war and to fight. A joyous person from being in the society of serious people may become serious, and a sad person from being with cheerful people may become cheerful. The soul acquires only those qualities in which it is interested; it will never take on those in which it is not interested. And the soul keeps only those attributes in which it is interested; it loses those in which it is not interested. However wicked a person may be, however many undesirable attributes he may have inherited, he can throw them all off by the power of will if he does not like them.

You will say, "But can we change our physical body, can we change our face?" We can. People become like those of whom they think strongly or with whom they associate. I have seen herdsmen, who live with the cattle and sheep, and from association with the cattle and sheep their faces had become very like the animals'. It is our thoughts and feelings that change our appearance, and if we had control over them we should develop that appearance that we wish to develop.

But for those who are walking in the path of Truth there is no heredity. By realizing their divine origin they free themselves from all earthly inheritance. As Christ said, "My Father in heaven," so they realize their origin from the spirit, and by their concentration and meditation they can create all the merits they wish for and clear away from their soul all influences which they do not like to possess.

Reincarnation

When we study religions, comparing them, we find that part of the world has believed in reincarnation, but most of the world has not held this belief. Krishna, Shiva, and Buddha are said to have taught the doctrine of reincarnation; Moses, Christ, and Mohammed have said nothing about it. This divides religions into two groups.

But when we make a deeper study we see that we can combine the two, for the tendency of the Sufi is rather to unite than to differ.

There are four widely-spread religions: Islam, Christianity, Brahminism, and Buddhism, which have great influence upon humanity by their diffusion. Let us ask each what it has to say on the matter.

Islam is silent on this subject, Christianity says nothing. In their scriptures if there may be rarely a verse which supports this idea there will be ten verses which disprove it.

Let us now consider Brahminism. There are four grades of Brahmins: *brahmachari, grihasta, vanaprasti,* and *sannyasi.* The three lower grades will perhaps answer, "Yes, there is reincarnation, but it depends upon our karma, our actions. If we, who are men, behave like animals, we may come again as animals, we may be a cow, or a dog, or a cat, or else we may be a human being of a lower order than we are now; and if we live a righteous life we shall find ourselves in a better condition in our next incarnation." When we ask the highest authority among Hindus, the *sannyasi*, he will say, "You will, perhaps, reincarnate, I shall not. I am *jivan mukta*, free; I am above the cycle of births and deaths."

Let us now see what Buddhism has to say. It says, "The world is in evolution; so we shall by no means become animals, but we evolve into higher and higher incarnations until we have overcome all weaknesses and have reached *nirvana*, perfection; then we return no more."

By this we see that there are only two believers in reincarnation, and even these two have contrary beliefs.

We read in the Bible (St. John xiv. 3), "I come again and will receive you unto myself," and (Acts i, 11), " . . . This Jesus which was received up from you into heaven, shall so come in like manner as ye beheld him going into heaven." This does not refer to the person of Christ, but to the innermost being of the Master, which was in reality the Being of God. If it concerned his person he would have said, "I shall come, but you also will come again, either in a better condition or in a worse state of being," but nothing of the kind is said. One might say, "Why then did the Master say 'I,' why did he not clearly say 'God'?" The answer is that divine personality is the losing of the thought of one's limited self, the absolute merging into the divine and only personality; then the ego becomes the divine ego, the "I" is not identification with the limited personality but with the personality of God. When Christ said "I," he meant God.

One reads the same in the *Masnavi* of Jelal-ud-Din Rumi, "Seventy-two forms I have worn and have come to witness this same spring of continual change." This also refers to the divine consciousness which wears various forms and comes to witness this world of changes; it is not the seventy-two times coming of

Maulana Rumi himself. Seventy-two is symbolical of many. Otherwise it would mean that since the human creation he visited the earth only seventy-two times, which would be very few times for such a great length of time.

There are many statements in the Koran such as these: "We will change their faces," said of the wicked, and "We will make them monkeys." The real meaning of the former is, "We will cause the brightness, or the happiness, of their expression to fade away by throwing light upon their hidden crimes which so long have kept them bright and happy"; it certainly does not mean, "We will make a Frenchman a Chinese." The meaning of the latter is, "They have imitated that which they were not." "They will be monkeys," means that they will be taken for that which they are in reality and not for that which they falsely pretended to be, in other words, "We will lay bare the mockery of the impostors."

In the Gospel we read (St. John ix. 1-3), " . . . as . . . Jesus . . . passed by he saw a man blind from his birth. And his disciples asked him, saying, Rabbi, did this man sin, or his parents, that he should be born blind? Jesus answered, Neither did this man sin, nor his parents; but that the works of God should be made manifest in him." This needs no interpretation, for it plainly says that the man's blindness was not the punishment of his former sins.

In the Koran it is written, "All are from God and return to Him." This denies a return to earth. Mention is made, however, of another life in the Surah, "Every soul must taste of death, and ye shall only be paid your reward in full on the resurrection day." Here the resurrection is spoken of, the making alive of the souls without the physical body, and it is plainly said that this existence will be as clear and distinct as is our life on earth.

As the world advances in intellectual development it becomes more and more interested in novelty; whatever is new is taken up and often the new idea is accepted and followed. The idea of re-incarnation has made a great impression in the present age, because it appeals at once to the scientific faculty and reasoning natures and it also satisfies those who wish to keep a fast hold on their individuality.

I remember, when in my early age I first knew of death, how for hours I became sad, thinking, "This, my body, the only means of experiencing life, will be one day in the grave. I shall be away from all things and beings that are the interest of life to me today. This whole environment which interests me and keeps me engaged all day long will be one day a mist; neither shall I see anybody nor will anybody see me; all whom I love today will be one day sepa-rated from me." Now my own experience in the past clearly tells me how others must feel at the idea of turning into what seems nothing after being something. It is just as it is when a dream interests us so much that if we wake up in the midst of it, and realize at once that we were dreaming, we yet like to close our eyes and give ourselves up to the enjoyment of the experience. Such is the case of all those who are so much interested in the dream of life that the idea of death, which is a more real state of being, is horrible to them. They would rather live a life unreal but individual than a life real but unrealized.

The idea of reincarnation often comforts those who think that it is too soon to renounce the pleasures of life in order to commune with God. "Perhaps," they say, "in our next life on earth we shall achieve what we have not achieved in this." Also it consoles those who have lost their loved ones, for they think these are not lost forever but will be born again, and often they look for them whenever a child is born among their acquaintance. It consoles those people also who have not obtained the fruit of their desires in this life and have always longed and hoped for something which could not be gained; these build their only hope on gaining the same in their next incarnation.

This idea often becomes a great hindrance to the real spiritual attainment, though it is helpful to a person who is discontented with his life, suffering from pain, poverty, or illness, and thinks that it is his karma to suffer this, and that then, when he has paid the uttermost farthing, his days will change. Then he has no more complaint to make; though he knows he has not committed in this life such sins as to be punished so, still he thinks that there is justice, as he has perhaps sinned in his past life. The idea seems reasonable, especially to a person who looks at life from a practical point of view. "Every man weighs the world on his own scales." And the thought of reincarnation is still more helpful to those who do not believe in God or know His being, also to those who neither believe in everlasting life nor can understand it. For some people it is very consoling to think that they will come on this earthly plane again and again, brought here by their karma, rather than to think, as many materialists do, "When we are dead we are done with forever."

The reason why the doctrine of reincarnation was taught to the Hindus and Buddhists must have been that the people of India at that time were very much developed intellectually, in philosophy, in science, in logic, in the material phenomena, and believed in law more than in love.

In the present age, especially in the West, people are beginning now to search for truth by the light of science and logic, as did the Hindus of the Vedic period. The peoples of India were working along the same lines at the origin of Brahminism and still more in the time of Buddhism.

Then, especially among the Mongolians, the people most advanced in arts and sciences, the enlightened were very logical and scientific, with little devotional tendency, and the masses had innumerable objects of worship. There the average person could not conceive the idea of the soul, the hereafter and God as it was propagated in another part of the East by the Hebrew prophets, so the theory of reincarnation was the best means of appealing to their reason instantly in order to break their former ideas. But as it is the nature of the human heart to worship someone, naturally their worship was directed to Buddha.

There is every probability that this idea came originally from the *devata*, the divine messengers born among Hindus. Each of these declared that he was the incarnation of Brahma, God, and each in turn claimed to be the reincarnation of the preceding *deva*, whom he succeeded. In claiming to be the incarnation of Brahma or the deva they succeeded, they did not mean that in their guise God was born or their predecessor reborn, but that they had realized God or that they possessed the same knowledge and mission as their predecessor. When the others asked him, "Of what are we the incarnations?" they were obliged to give them some explanation of a like kind, and they told each one that which his condition of life suggested to them.

When the four *varnas*, castes, were made in India—*Brahmin, Kshattria, Vayesha,* and *Kshuddra*—these were not in fact different castes but classes. The whole administration was arranged in this way: Brahmins to study, meditate, and be worshipped, Kshattrias to fight and guard the country, Vayeshas to carry on commerce, and Kshuddras to labor and serve. None save Brahmins had *adhicar*, the right to study the Vedas, the books of mysticism and philosophy; even Kshattrias and Vayeshas had to be content in the worship of the Brahmins and with the Purana, the religion taught in legends; Kshuddras, the laboring class, were denied even that.

It has always been the tendency of the stronger and more intelligent men to keep the weak and simple down. Owing to the inclination of the higher caste to keep itself pure from further admixture of the lower classes, a religious rule was made enforcing the belief that the Kshuddra, the lowest, could not become a Vayesha, the Vayesha could not become a Kshattria, nor a Kshattria be admitted among Brahmins, the highest and supreme class of the time, unless by his good actions he had made it possible that he should be born, in the next incarnation, in a family of the higher caste. The idea of reincarnation, as a belief generally held, was made the basis of the Hindu religion, upon which the whole building of Brahminism was erected. But everyone in the world has an inclination to raise his head and climb up higher, if he can, from that level upon which he may have been set in life. Verily the light of truth, the beauty of nature, the desire for freedom, the idea of unity cannot be covered; sooner or later it flashes forth.

The law of *karma*, action, is the philosophy which a reasoning brain holds in support of reincarnation, saying, "There is no such being as God as an intervener in our life's affairs, but it is we who by our actions produce results similar to them. There is the ever-ruling law of cause and effect; therefore, every occurrence in life must be in accordance with it. If we do not get the results of our good or wicked deeds immediately, that is because they need time to mature so as to produce similar results; if they do not in this life, then the law drags us to be born again in another incarnation, in order to experience in that the effect of our deeds."

Looking at the wheel of evolution one sees that we do not always rise, we also fall. We do not always become better people; sometimes man grows worse than he was. The nature of evolution is like a wheel turning round, not rising always. This gives us reason to doubt how far the Buddhistic idea of better and better reincarnations can prove to be logical.

In support of reincarnation a story is told of two friends who were going out for a holiday. One said, "Let us go to the temple; there we shall hear the name of God, we shall be uplifted." The other said, "You are always such a melancholy boy; you always find such dull occupations. We will not go to the temple, we will go where we can enjoy ourselves; we will go to the Gaiety." The first said, "I do not like that idea, I will not go with you." So they parted. The one who went to the temple on his way met with an accident from a wagon in the road and his foot was crushed. He thought, "What a good thing that my friend did not come with me; he too would have been injured." The other on his way to the Gaiety had great luck, he found a purse full of gold coins. He thought, "Thank God! If my friend had been with me, I should have had to share this with him." As soon as the first had re-covered a little, he went to a Brahmin and asked him, "What was the reason that I, who was on my way to the temple, had the bad luck to have my foot crushed, and my friend, who was on his way to the Gaiety, had the good luck that he found this gold purse?" The Brahmin said, "The reason is that you in your former life did some very bad action, and you were meant to be killed, and not only killed but hanged for everybody to see, but it happened that only your foot was crushed. Your friend in his former life did some very good action and he was meant to be a king, but it happened for his present sins that he only found a purse full of gold coins."

If we believe in the idea we must first understand where evil ends and where good begins. It has never been possible for a deep thinker to draw a line between good and evil. What distinction do we find, from this point of view, between good and evil, if it be seen with a magnifying view? None but the difference of degree and difference of view. What seems good to one person to the other does not, and so it is with evil. Also every evil to the eye of the seer is a lesser good, which in comparison with the greater good appears different from that and so is called evil.

And if the wheel of births and deaths depends upon cause and effect, I should say it must go on forever and ever and there would never be an end to it. According to this doctrine not only the punishment of our sins, but even the reward of the good we have done would drag us back to earth; we shall have to come back on earth in any case. Even should we not wish for a reward we cannot stop the wheel, for we have no power over nature's law. What a helpless condition! Neither does God intervene in our affairs, that He might stop it with His all-might, nor can we, helpless human beings subject to the law of cause and effect.

Again considering this subject we see that everything existing can be destroyed by some other thing or substance. There is no stain that cannot be cleaned off by some chemical solution. There is no record which cannot be erased from the surface of the paper, even if it is engraved upon stone it can be scraped off. Man, the master of the whole creation, has found the means to destroy all things, and it is very astonishing if he is unable to find a solution to wipe off the impressions of karma, life's deeds, so as to escape the wheel of births and deaths, when he professes to know all things of the earth and claims to have solved all the mysteries of the heavens.

Some believers in God say in support of reincarnation, "God is just. There are many who are lame or blind or unhappy in life, and this is the punishment for the faults they have committed before, in a former incarnation. If it were not so, that would be injustice on the part of God." That makes God only a reckoner and not a lover, and it restricts Him to his justice like a judge bound by the law. The judge is the slave of law, the forgiver is its master. In fact we ourselves, limited as we are, have mercy in us, so that often if someone has done something against us we forgive. If he only bows before us we say, "He has humiliated himself, I will forget." I have seen mothers who, even if their son has caused them much sorrow, if, when he has any trouble, he only says, "Mother, I have done this, but you are the one to whom I can come for sympathy," will say, "My child, I forgive you, though at the time it made me sad." If we, who are full of faults and errors, having in us that little spark of mercy inherited from God, can forgive, how can we think that God, the most merciful, will reckon our faults like a judge? We are as little children before Him.

Regarding God as a personal being, how can we think that He, Whose being is love, Whose action is love, Who is all love, can weigh our actions as a judge would?

A judge, also, when someone is brought before him, after he has looked into the case, says, "I have looked into your case and I find that you are guilty. You are given six months', or five years', or ten years' imprisonment. Your fault is very bad and so you must learn not to do it again." But if we go to the blind and lame and ask them, "Were you given this in punishment? Were you told so?" they say, "No, we were told nothing." Now how are we to imagine that God could be so unjust as to punish them and yet not tell them of their crime?

If we return, then every child that is born should know what he was before. If only exceptional ones feel that they know what they were before, in another life, then it may be a delusion, a pretense, or a scheme for gaining notoriety by appearing to know what everybody does not know.

If God is most merciful how could he govern us only by law void of love and compassion, when even we human beings forget and forgive another's fault in spite of law, reason and logic, when moved by love, our divine inheritance? "God is love," not law. Love in its lower manifestation turns into law by forming habits, yet it is not law which rules love, it is love that controls law.

The idea of forgiveness is the result of our idealizing God. As we idealize God, so he proves to be. Sometimes the sins of a whole life may be wiped off in one instant; sometimes all the virtue and piety of a whole life may be lost by one sin.

A story is told that Moses was going to Mount Sinai and on his way he met a very pious person, who said to him, "Moses, speak to God of me. All my life I have been pious, I have been virtuous, I have prayed to God, and I have had nothing but troubles and misfortunes." A little later Moses met a man sitting in the street with a bottle of liquor. He called out, "Moses! Where are you going?" Moses said, "To Mount Sinai." The man called out, "To Mount Sinai? Then speak to God of me," for he was drunk.

Moses went to Mount Sinai and he told God of the pious person whom he had met. God said, "For him there is a place in the heavens." Then he told God of the drunken man whom he had met. God said, "He shall be sent to the worst possible place in hell."

Moses went away and first he met the drunken man. He told him, "God says you shall be sent to the worst possible place in hell." The man said, "God spoke of me?" and he was so overjoyed that he could not contain himself but began to dance, just as a poor man might be overjoyed if he heard that a king had spoken of him, even if the king had said nothing good of him. Then he said, "How happy should I be that He, the Creator and Sovereign of the universe, knows me, the great sinner." Then Moses told the pious person what God had said. He said, "Why not? I have spent all my life in the worship of God and in piety, sacrificing all else in life; and therefore I am entitled to have it."

Both the pious person and the drunkard died, and Moses was curious to know what had become of them. He went to Mount Sinai and asked God. God said, "The pious person is in hell, and the drunken man is in heaven." Moses thought, "Does God break his word?" God said, "The drunkard's joy on hearing that We had spoken of him has wiped out all his sins. The pious person's virtue was worthless. Why could he not be satisfied if We made the sun shine and sent the rain?"

If anyone were to weigh his righteous actions against the myriad favors of God, all the righteous actions of every moment of his life would not compare with one moment of God's favor. Therefore the devotee forgets his righteous actions, looking only at the favor of God. "When the pious was looking for the beloved God among the righteous, His mercy cried out, 'Come hither. I am busy among sinners, forgiving them their sins' " (Amir).

Man, the Seed of God

Man may most justly be called the seed of God. God the infinite, most conscious within Himself, embraces His nature full of variety; in this way He is one and He is all. The whole manifestation is just like a tree sprung from the divine root. Nature is like its stem and all the aspects of nature are like the branches, the leaves, the fruit, and the flower, and from this tree again the same seed is produced, the human soul, which was the first cause of the tree. This seed is the spirit of man, and as God comprehends the whole universe within Himself, being one, so man contains within himself the whole universe as His miniature. "In our own image we have created man" (Koran). Therefore neither can God be anything else than what He is, for the very reason that He is one and at the same time He is all. Nor can man; neither can man be reincarnated nor can God.

The men of science today have admitted the fact that all the skin of man is changed in so many years and they have been able is identified. Again, in our food and drink we live upon so many times in life, renewing his body each time. If the body is subject to change, so is the mind, and it is only by these that man's person is identified. Again, in our food and drink we life upon so many small lives and so many small lives live upon us, dwelling in our blood, veins, tubes, and in the skin, all of which constitutes our individuality. And in the mind our every thought and feeling is as alive as we, even such beings as the elementals, demons, and angels, which are created within us, from us, and of us, and yet may as fitly be called individuals as we. So in the end of the examination it is hard for a man to find whether he exists as one or many.

In our dreams all the inhabitants of our mind resurrect, forming a world within ourselves. We see in the dream things and beings, a friend, a foe, an animal, a bird, and they come from nowhere, but are created out of our own selves. This shows that the mind of an individual constitutes a world in itself, which is created and destroyed by the conscious or unconscious action of the will, which has two aspects, intention and accident. We have experience of this world of mind even while awake, but the contrast between the world within and without makes the world without concrete and the world within abstract.

Someone may ask, "If all that we see in the dream is we ourselves then why do we even in the dream see ourselves as an entity separate from all other things before us in the dream?" The answer is, "Because the soul is deluded by our external form, and this picture it recognizes as I, and all other images and forms manifesting before it in the dream stand in contrast to this I; therefore the soul recognizes them as other than I."

Therefore, if it is one individual that reincarnates, should we hold our changeable body to be an individual or our mind, both of which appear to be one and at the same time many? One might ask Jack, "Which part of yourself is Jack, the eye, the nose, the ear, or the hand or foot, each of which has a particular name? Or are your thoughts and feelings Jack? They are numerous, changeable, and diverse; you name them as such an imagination, such a feeling." This shows that Jack stands aloof as the owner of all the finer and grosser properties that have grouped and formed an illusion before him, which, reflected upon his soul, makes him say, "I, Jack." He is the owner of all that he realizes around and about him, and yet each atom and vibration which has composed his illusionary self is liable to change, to a separate and individual birth and death.

The soul on its journey to the infinite cannot turn back halfway; and when it reaches that goal, it experiences only the light, the wisdom, the love of God, and it loses two things: it loses all the marks of the experiences and thoughts of its manifestation and it gradually loses its individuality and merges in the infinite, divine consciousness.

If an earthen thing is thrown into the water it has a tendency to go to the bottom, to its own element. If water is accompanying fire on its journey, its water part still drips down as steam. When fire travels with the air it takes its smoke so far, but in its higher spheres it gets rid of the fire. When ether turns into spirit it drops its contact with the air element. Thus it is with the soul; on its return journey it gives back all the above properties to their own sources, thus lightening its load on its way towards its own element. The earthly body goes to earth, its water part to the world of waters, its heat to the kingdom of heat, its air to the spheres of the air, its ether into the ethereal regions. Its impressions, thoughts, feelings, merits, qualities go as far as they can reach, and remain at their stations, wherever they are meant to be. Then it is the soul in its own essence that is left, merging into the ocean of consciousness where nothing of its previous property remains.

Our personality is just like a bubble in the water. As little probability as there is of a bubble once merged in the sea coming out again composed of the same portion of water, so little probability is there for the soul once merged in the ocean of consciousness to come out again formed of the self-same portion of consciousness. The bubble may come back in the same place with the same portion of water, or it may be another portion of water. There may be half of the first drop of water in the second bubble, there may be a small part, or there may be some portion of water added to it.

If one bubble comes, and we call that bubble John and then we call another Jacob and a third Henry, yet they are all the same water, and if we call the water John they are all the same John. All is the same spirit, the same life, involving itself into all the forms and the names. From this point of view there is no I, no you, no he, no she, no it, in the light of reality; all are but the differences of a moment.

Every bubble loses both reflections or any properties it possessed during its existence as soon as it merges in the water, and if once in a thousand chances it should come formed of the self-same portion of water, it would not retain its previous property. In the same way supposing, as a mere assumption, that the self-same portion of consciousness, which, in the first place, is not so substantial and stable as water, could possibly appear again on the surface without any addition or deduction, it is utterly impossible that it should still possess its past qualities and impressions, for it has been absolutely purified by sinking into the consciousness. And if even a drop of ink loses its ink property in the sea, why should not the ocean of consciousness purify its own element from all elements foreign to itself?

As Hinduism teaches the doctrine that bathing once in the Sangum at the confluence of the two rivers can purify man from all life's sins, how can it deny that this bath of the soul, sinking into the consciousness even once, purifies the soul from all the properties it has gathered during its previous life? In the first place, the nature itself of absorption in the Spirit is purification from the material state of being, and the very nature of manifestation is for the soul to come new and fresh.

Suppose we grant that cream is the reincarnation of milk and butter is the third step of the reincarnation of milk and its fourth reincarnation may be called ghee; then the question arises, of what is milk the reincarnation? Milk is composed of several chemical substances, and its chemical arrangement changes the name, savor, smell, and effect. Butter cannot be called milk, nor is ghee cream. If there is anything which seems to be existing through all the manifestation of the milk, it is the inner ruling current which groups and scatters atoms, compelling them to change, which may be likened to the soul.

Also, if Jack has reincarnated as John, or John has reincarnated as Jack, what were both in the beginning? Were they two or one? If one became two, then one could become thousands, millions, and still he is one only.

The shooting forth of the soul from the consciousness can be symbolized as an arrow. The arrow shot up in the air goes up as far as the will and power of the sender has destined it to go, and when it reaches its uttermost height its return begins. The death of the physical being is the return of that arrow. Of course, on its return it may be detained on its way, perhaps, as the arrow is sometimes caught in the branches of a tree, but it returns some day or other to the earth, its own element. It does not go up again from there by any means. So it is with the human soul, which, after finishing its course on earth, returns to its origin, drawn by its power of attraction.

When we look at the world we see that everything makes a circle. The plant grows from the seed to its developed state and returns to dust. Man grows from childhood to youth, to maturity, then to old age. This, it is said, is an argument for our passing through many lives. But it is not the circle which journeys, but the point which, journeying, forms the circle and returns to the place from which it started. It is the consciousness that performs the journey and not the individual soul.

The drops of water in a fountain go up, some higher, some lower, some go a very little way, some rise very high. When each drop falls down it sinks into the stream, flowing away with it and does not rise again, although the water of the same stream rises again and falls again in drops, which proves to us the fact that the water rises and falls continually, not the drop; yet apparently it rises and falls as drops, though the portion of water in every drop is different.

One point which the reincarnationists hold in support of their doctrine is the traces of unusual genius or gift found in a child who does not seem to inherit the same from his ancestors and cannot acquire it from his surroundings. Sometimes in the slums a child is born which has great poetical genius which could not be found in its father or mother nor in its forefathers, or a great musical gift which could not be found in its father or grandfather or ancestors.

The soul before its coming on the face of the earth for a very, very long time, on its way to manifestation, gathers the impressions of those souls whom it meets on its way and takes on their attributes. In this way the attributes of the past ones are manifested again. A soul may receive the impressions of one soul or of a few souls or of many souls.

The soul on its way toward manifestation may meet the soul of a genius in poetry or music and take with it these impressions. When some very great or very good or philanthropic person has died you will find that soon after a child of like qualities will be born to balance the world. A child may be born with the qualities of Alexander the Great. This is because the new soul coming out towards manifestation has met the soul of Alexander and has become impressed with all his qualities or part of his qualities. Such a one may assert, "I am the reincarnation of Alexander." But the soul of Alexander does not return. If it did, then every soul that has left this life would know of his former lives.

Much of the difference of understanding is the difference of words. If someone says that the soul is the world of impressions which the consciousness holds before it and the spirit is the consciousness, then he may say that the soul returns.

When the child of unpoetical parents sings, making up words of its own, this shows that it has received the impression of some poetical soul. The soul that comes to the surface is more responsive than creative; it is not creative, because it has nothing to give. The soul on its return is creative; it imparts its experiences there. For example, an unused photographic plate takes the impression of the object before it, but the used plate reflects its impression on to the paper. Suppose, for instance, the soul of Vishnu meets a soul on its way to manifestation, this powerful soul may impress the other with its attributes. Then that soul may say, "I am Krishna, the reincarnation of Vishnu." The soul is impressed with whatever comes before it. Sometimes children of quite ordinary parents may be so impressed by a great person in whose presence they are that they themselves become great. And as man's personality is nothing but an agglomeration of his thoughts and impressions, the inheritor of that may be called the reincarnation of the past one, although his soul is his own.

Sometimes a child appears to see and understand very much of what is going on around him from his infancy. Sometimes a young man sees and understands more than an old person. Such people are supposed by the average person to be old souls, and the reincarnationists take it as a proof of the doctrine of reincarnation. But, really speaking, knowing and understanding do not depend upon learning; knowledge is the soul's quality. The knowledge of the spirit has been man's in all ages. An old person does not need to read many books in order to learn that he was once a little child; he knows it, it is his past experience. So the soul knows its own experience; it needs only a little awakening to make it self-conscious.

When the Shah of Persia wished to have the history of Persia written by some literary person there was no one found who could do it until the mystical poet Firdausi said that he would write it. And he wrote, from his inner knowledge, the *Shah-Namah*, the history of the Shahs of Persia. If he had this knowledge from the recollection of his own previous lives he must have reincarnated repeatedly in Persia and in Persia only, uninterruptedly, endowed each time with the same degree of intelligence, so as to acquire and retain all this knowledge.

There is nothing which the soul cannot know, for the whole objective existence is made by the soul for its own use, and therefore it is not astonishing if man possesses great qualities that he has not inherited, and if he has knowledge of all things through revelation, not by learning. It is astonishing only when he lacks this, and that is owing to the globes upon globes of the objective world covering the light of the soul.

I first believed without any hesitation in the existence of the soul, and then I wondered about the secret of its nature. I persevered and strove in search of the soul, and found at last that I myself was the cover over my soul. I realized that that which believed in me, and that which wondered in me, and that which persevered in me, and that which found in me, and that which was found at last was no other than my soul. I thanked the darkness that brought me to the light, and I valued the veil which prepared for me the vision in which I saw myself reflected, the vision produced in the mirror of my soul. Since then I have seen all souls as my soul and realized my soul as the soul of all, and what bewilderment it was when I realized that I alone was, if there were anyone, and I am whatever and whoever exists, and I shall be whoever there will be in the future, and there was no end to my happiness and joy. Verily, I am the seed and I am the root and I am the fruit of this tree of life.

Akibat
Life After Death

Death

We love our body so much and identify ourselves with it, so that we are very unhappy to think that this our body, which is so dear to us, will be some day in the grave. No one likes to think that it will die and be destroyed.

The soul is our true self. It existed before our birth and will exist after our death. That which holds the conception of "I," a living entity, is not the body but the soul deluded by the body. The soul thinks that it is the body; it thinks that it walks, sits, lies down when the body does. Really it does none of these things. A little indisposition of the body makes it think, "I am ill." A little offense makes it dejected. A little praise makes it think itself in heaven. Really it is not in heaven nor on earth, it is where it is. The soul's dwelling in the material body deludes it so much that it thinks, "I can live only on material food, can stand only on earth, can enjoy only material surroundings. Without this I am nowhere. I am nothing."

There is a Persian verse, "Do not build a house on the ground of another." This is what the soul does. Whatever it sees, the consciousness recognizes as itself. Its purity makes it reflect whatever is before it, and then it thinks, "This is I," just as clear water reflects your image. The soul then wants to have everything very good and very nice for its comfort and vanity. It wants to see its objective self very well dressed, then it wants very good things about it. It sets up a very good house, and all this life it is in pursuit of these things. Then, when death comes, this building raised on the sand is blown away. Its gathered property is taken from it. This is a very, very great disappointment. All that in which it takes interest, it loses. Its withdrawing into its pure self, and the scattering of all earth's deluding environments from its sight, impresses it with the idea of death to its greatest horror. This horror and this disappointment are the only death there is, for the body is nothing but a covering put over our soul, and when it is gone we are not dead; just as we do not think that we are dead when our coat is worn out, or if someone tears our shirt.

The moment when a person dies is the only moment when he feels that he is dead. Then the impression of his dying condition, the hopelessness of the doctor, the sorrow and grief of the family, all make up this impression. After death, as he recovers from this impression, he gradually finds himself alive, for the life which kept him alive with his physical garb of course feels strange in its absence, yet it is not dead. It is even more alive, for its great burden has been removed, which for a time had made him think that the physical garb was his life.

The soul by its power has created from itself, and has attracted from outside, the elements, and collected them, and it holds them; but by its utilizing them they are gradually worn out, and last only for a certain period. The soul holds the body composed of all these elements so long as it has interest in the body, and so long as the magnetism of the body holds it and its activity keeps it engaged. As soon as its interest in the body is lessened, or the elements that form the body have lost their power by feebleness, or some irregularity in the system, the body loosens its hold, and the soul, whose innate inclination is to free itself, takes advantage of this opportunity that the bodily inability gives it. The result of this is death.

"Then," you may say, "this is all, and after death there will be nothing for the ordinary person who has realized himself as this body, so tall, so broad, so heavy, his age so many years?"

You may say, "Then when the physical body is gone, all is gone." But it is not so; when the body is gone the mind remains, the finer part of man's self, composed of vibrations. The elements exist in the vibrations as well as in the atoms. If not, a person who is angry would not get red and hot. In the dream, when the body is asleep, we see ourselves walking, speaking, acting, in such surroundings, with such people. It is only by the contrast with the waking condition that we call it a dream. This self still exists after the body is gone, the exact counterpart of what we are now: not of what we were when we were five years old, or ten years old, but of what we are now.

If it is said that the soul is that which remains after the death of the physical body, and that is it then in heaven or in hell, that is not so. The soul is something much greater. How can that be burned with fire which is itself light, *nur*, the light of God? But owing to its delusion, it takes upon itself all the conditions that the mind has to go through after death. Therefore the experience after death of the soul that has not attained to liberation is very depressing. If the mind is not much attached to the earthly life and has gathered the satisfaction of its deeds, it enjoys heaven; if the contrary, then it experiences hell.

The mind that is more involved in the earthly cares and attachments cannot let the soul be in the light. If you throw an air-balloon into the air it will go up and then it will come down again. It goes up because of the air that is in it, it comes down because of the earth substance in it. The tendency of the soul is to go to the highest spheres, to which it belongs; that is its nature. The earthly substance it has gathered around it weighs it down to earth. The kite goes up, but the string in a person's hand brings it back to earth. The earthly attachments are the string that draws the soul downwards. We see that the smoke goes up and on its way it leaves in the chimney its earth substance. All the rest of its earth substance it leaves in the air, and until it has left all behind, it cannot go up to the ether. By this simile we see how the soul cannot rise from the lower regions until it has left behind all earthly longings and attachments.

Man has a great fear of death, and especially the simple, tender, and affectionate people, and those people who are very much attached to their father and mother and brothers and sisters and friends, to their positions and possessions. But also those who are unfortunate in life fear death. A person will rather be very ill than dead. He will rather be in the hospital than in the grave with the dead people. When the thought comes to man, "Some day I must leave all this and go in the grave," a great sadness comes. With some people this fear lasts for a part of the life; with some it lasts the whole life. The proof of how great the fear of death is, is that death has been made the worst punishment, although it is not nearly so bad as the pains, sorrows, and worries in life.

Death is the great examination, to which one goes prepared, another unprepared, one with confidence, another with fear. However much anyone may pretend to be spiritual or virtuous in life, at the sight of death he is tested and all pretense falls away. "Then, when the crushing calamity shall come, on that day shall man remember what he has striven after" (Koran).

An old man was always crying and lamenting, saying, "I am so unhappy, my life is so hard, every day toil and labor. It would be better if I were dead." Every day he lamented in this way and called upon death to come and take him. One day Azrael, the angel of death, appeared and said to him, "You have called me so often, now I am come to take you with me." The old man said, "Not yet! I am an old man, pray grant me only a few days more of life." The angel of death said, "No. You have so often asked to die, and now you must come to Allah." The old man said, "Wait a little while. Let me stay here a little longer." But the angel of death said, "Not one moment more," and he carried him off.

What thought should the mind hold at the moment of death? The thought should be, in accordance with the evolution of the person, either of God, or of the object of his devotion, or of pleasant surroundings and whatever he likes and has idealized. If he is an earthly person then the thought of pleasant surroundings will make a heaven for him. If he is in a state of devotion, he will unite with the object of his devotion. If he is godly, the thought of God will be right for him. "Verily death is the bridge which unites friend to friend" (Koran).

Those of whom it is said that they are in the presence of God, are those who hold the vision of their divine Beloved whom they have idealized all their life, and they rejoice for a very, very long time in the presence of their idealized One.

During our life on earth we are conscious of three conditions, that of the body, mind, and soul. After the physical death we are conscious of two only. On the physical plane, if the thief comes, we are not so much afraid. We look to find with what we could attack him. But in the dream we are afraid, for we have nothing with which to attack him. Here the will is much stronger. There the imagination is stronger, and the will less. In the physical life we have the change from one experience to another. If in the night we are afraid, we say, "I had a nightmare, but it means nothing." We say, "In the dream I was sad, but it means nothing." There we have no change.

Therefore it is here that we should awaken to what is the aim of our life. There we cannot improve so much as we can here.

Therefore there have always been some, the chosen ones of God, who have said, "Awake, awake, while it is time."

There are some who in the dream can do what they wish. They can make happen what they will, and the next day they see that happen which they saw in the night. Such are exceptional cases. Because they have mastered their will here, they can make all things go according to their will even in the higher plane. When a person is just as glad that another should eat a good dish as he should eat it himself, that another should wear a beautiful dress as he should wear it himself, then he is raised above humanity. These are the saints and sages, and their hereafter is in their hands, because they are happy both in the gain and loss.

The mind of the prophets and murshids cannot be compared with other minds. Theirs is a master mind, and they can hold it much longer. As they have lived only for others, after death they still live for others. They have thought only of what is eternal. Others have thought of things that pass away, and so in time their mind passes away.

It is usually for this reason that Sufism is learned, that a person may know what will happen to him after death, in that being which is our real being, and yet ordinarily is hidden from us.

After the physical death the life that cannot be dead bears man up and he is always alive. Both on earth and sea we living beings exist, having both elements in our form, the earth and the water. The beings of the sea are formed of earth also; we have water also in our constitution. Yet the sea is as strange to us as earth to the creatures of the sea. Both would not like their places exchanged, and if it so happens that they are out of their place, it leads them to their end. It is because the fish has not realized that it is an earthly being and earth is its place too, that it cannot live on earth, and in the same way beings on land fail when they think that they will be sunk in the sea, whose relief lies in getting to the shore.

If we were dropped into the sea, it would be a terrible thing. We should be sure that, "I shall go to the bottom, I shall be drowned." It is our fear that makes us go to the bottom and our thought; except for this there is no reason why we should sink. The sea lifts up the whole ship in which a thousand people are travelling, upon which tons of weight are loaded; why should it not lift up our little body?

Our inner being is like the sea, our external being as the earth. So it is with the word called death. It is the sea part of ourselves, where we are taken from our earth part, and, not being accustomed to it, we find the journey unfamiliar and uncomfortable, and call it death. To the seaman the sea is as easy to journey upon, whenever he chooses to, as the land. Christ, in connection with this subject, said to Peter, "O thou of little faith, wherefore didst thou doubt?" In the Sanskrit and Prakrit both, liberation is called *taran*, meaning swimming. It is swimming which makes water the abode of the earthly fish, and for those who swim in the ocean of eternal life, in the presence and in the absence of the body, it becomes their everlasting abode.

The swimmer plays with the sea. At first he swims a little way, then he swims far out. Then he masters it. Then it is his home, his element, as the earth is. He who has mastered these two elements has gained all mastery.

The divers in the port of Ceylon, and the Arabs in the Red Sea dive down into the sea. First they stop up their ears, eyes, lips, and their nose, then they dive and they bring up pearls. The mystic also dives into the sea of consciousness by closing his senses from the external world and thus entering into the abstract plane.

The work of the Sufi is to take away the fear of death. This path is trodden in order to know in life what will be with us after death. The Koran says: "*Mutu kubla anta mutu*—Die before death."

To take off this mortal garb, to teach the soul that it is not this mortal but that immortal being, so that we may escape that great disappointment of mortality which death brings, this is what is accomplished in life by a Sufi.

The Day of Judgment

In Buddhism and in the Hindu religion there is little to be found said about the Day of Judgment because they have the doctrine of karma, but in the Koran it recurs so often in the different Surahs, and great emphasis is put upon it, and in the Bible the Day of Judgment is spoken of very many times.

This Day of Judgment, of which the religions have spoken, is a great secret. All that can be said about it is that not one moment of time, not the blinking of the eyes passes, without a judgment, that in the conscience of each individual there is the faculty of judging, which judges himself and others, and this faculty exists in its perfection in the universal conscience, which judges the whole universe. The former is man's justice, the latter the justice of God.

In man's justice partiality and error are found, for his conscience is overshadowed by his person; thus the seeing faculty of the conscience is dimmed. God's justice is the right justice, for no partial shadow falls upon his universal consciousness because the whole universe is his field of vision and therefore his sight is keen. As our justice determines our likes and dislikes and creates in us favor or disfavor for another, so it is with God. He reckons the account of deeds and bestows rewards and awards punishments, and also forgives by his mercy and compassion whomever he may choose for forgiveness, as do we human beings in our small way. To the shortsighted, man's justice is plain, but God's justice is too vague to be apprehended, and there are many examples to lead him astray, such as the righteous being ill-treated while the wicked enjoy life, but the keensighted can see the term of the enjoyment of the wicked and that of the ill-treatment of the righteous. The seer can see the blow waiting its time to fall upon the one, and the reward being prepared for the other. It is only a matter of time.

To a material person it seems absurd. He thinks, "If I rob someone, if the police catch me, that is the judgment. If they do not catch me, it is all right; then I am safe from it. If I have a purse full of money, and I can pay barristers and pleaders, it is all right." Because he does not see anything in the hereafter; he sees only what he is here.

A simple believer believes that there is a Day of Judgment, but he knows scarcely anything about it. Then it is for the Sufi to understand that there is a record of every action, thought, and work in the memory, nature's manuscript open before our own conscience, and if a murderer escapes the police, he cannot escape from his conscience within. One might think, "It is his own conscience, what does it matter if it is displeased awhile?" No; but there is the universal conscience behind it, perfectly just and all-powerful, which can hang him even by the waves of the sea, as a penalty for his crime, if he escaped from the land and sought refuge in the water.

Everything that we do, all our works, have three parts: the beginning, the action, and the end. In the beginning there is hope, in the action there is joy, but in the end comes the realization.

In the morning when one wakes up, he is fresh and ready to plan all the work of the day. All day a person works and in the evening he sees what result he has got by his work, how much he has gained.

When a child is born he is fresh and ready to enjoy everything. With any little thing, any little doll that is given, he is happy. He does not know where the world is nor what the cares of life are. Then he has to go through all experiences, good and bad, in life. When old age comes, then he sees the result of his action. At the time of action he does not see, because action is blinding. Then, if he has worked for riches, he has got riches. If he has worked for fame, now he has that. And if he loves, he receives the affection and sympathy of his surroundings. When he is old, that is the period of his judgment on earth. Then he sees the reward of his action. If he has murdered someone, the judgment is when he is hanged. If he has robbed, he is in jail and he repents. But the time of action comes only once, and after that it is too late to repair one's fault.

There are many things that we do that at the moment seem all right, but afterwards our self is not satisfied. It is just as when a person eats something that at the time has a pleasant taste, but afterwards it produces a bad odor, so that the smell of his own mouth makes his head ache. Whatever was tolerated in him so long as he had power, magnetism, and activity, together with his energy, his manner, his appearance, his looks, when the power has left him, no one will tolerate. He has become cranky. His children want to leave him, because they say that old papa has lost his head. His friends despise him, because they say that he is no use.

There are many habits and weaknesses of the mind which in youth do not seem of much consequence, such as jealousy, greed, envy, anger, and passion. When youth is gone, and the strength and magnetism of youth, then only weakness remains, with its gaping mouth. Whilst we are in the activity, we are blind. Our eyes are opened when the result comes.

A Badishah was once riding in the jungle. When crossing a bridge he saw a man who was quite drunk standing in the middle of the bridge. The man called out, "Will you sell that horse, O passerby?" for he was quite drunk and could not recognize the rider. The Badishah thought, "He is drunk," so he gave no heed. After shooting for some hours in the jungle he returned and saw the man who had been standing in the middle of the road now sitting by the roadside. The Badishah asked in fun of the man, "Do you want to purchase this horse?" The man's drunkenness was now passed. He was astonished to think what he had said to the Badishah in his drunken spell. But fortunately he thought of a very witty answer. He said, "The purchaser of the horse is gone, the groom of the horse remains." This amused the Badishah, who overlooked his fault.

There is a time when our ego desires all that tempts it, but when that stage of beginning and action is past, helplessness remains. Our life has three parts, the part before our birth, the time of our life, and the time after death.

When considering our life here and hereafter we understand that our life on earth is our youth, the hereafter age, the time of reaping the fruits of our actions. And the judgment comes in age, which is the time after death.

In the arts we see that there are these three aspects. In music there is first the introduction, then there is the music in its full grandeur, then there is the conclusion which gives the essence of all that has gone before. In painting, the artist first designs, then he colors the picture, and then he looks at it; if it is not as he likes, he wipes it off or he tears it up. A person might say, "You yourself have made it, why do you tear it up?" It is because he looks at it, and then sometimes he says, "This is valueless;" and when it is better, the artist desires it to be sent to the exhibition, and he proudly calls his relations and friends to look at it. This world is the Creator's picture. The Creator as an artist looks at his work and He alters it, improves it, or He wipes it off, as He chooses best.

Why is the Day of Judgment called "day"? Now I will explain why it is called the Day of Judgment, whether it is a day of twenty-four hours or a day of twelve hours or what. One day is when we are awake, our night is when we are asleep. It is not the day and night of the earth, which are limited to twelve hours each, but it is the day and night of the consciousness. What separates one day from another, what makes us distinguish the days, is the night.

Here our life is in the darkness of activity, where the world of illusion appears to our eyes as real and the rapid passing of life appears to us stable, just as when the train runs it appears to us as if the trees on the way were running while the train was standing still. When the illusionary life has proved to be not so real as we had thought it for some time, then comes the day, when things appear as clear as in daylight. To some few this comes in this world, but to all in the hereafter.

Here we have two states, the waking and the dream. There will be only the dream as the reality. That will be our day, uninterrupted by any intervening night. It will not change. And this day will last forever, meaning until our individuality is merged in the consciousness.

We dream of all things which are in our surroundings and all things as they naturally appear. We dream of a horse or an elephant or of our brother or sister or our mother, our father, or our uncle, but we do not dream of inexistent objects, such as a horse with wings or a rabbit with elephant's ears, because that is not our world.

That with which our consciousness is impressed, that only is our world. And that world comes into the judgment which is always going on. The world of the husbandman will be his cottage with his family; the world of the king will be the surroundings of his palace.

You will say, "Shall we not be in a great gathering where there will be millions and billions of souls in whatever form they may appear, and all the souls that have existed on earth will be tried at the same time?" It will be in appearance, but not in reality, for every individual's Judgment Day will reflect the whole world within himself and will be peculiar to himself—in other words, a world will be resurrected in each soul. The affirming and denying aspects of conscience—both will be in full play, sometimes in the guise of Munkir and Nakir, the recording angels.

In reality it will be like a talking-machine record put to the test, which repeats all one's life's known and forgotten, good and bad experiences, with the moving picture of all who were concerned with it, whether dead before or after or still alive on earth, which takes place before one's own soul in the presence of the perfectly just and mighty Being, the thorough knower and weigher of all things.

Heaven and Hell

The idea of heaven and hell exists in some form or other in all religions, which gives the religions a great hold upon the masses to keep them completely under their sway, inducing them to do good and to keep from evil, which without this becomes almost impossible, for man is always being tempted to evil, and great difficulties stand in his way when he attempts to do good, when the wicked seem to possess the kingdom of the earth, while the righteous are at the mercy of God. If no such promise were given, no other reward, however great, would ever have united mankind in the religion of faith.

The reward that God gives is quite different from any earthly comforts and riches, but in early times, and even before average people now, it could be expressed only in the form of earthly rewards. "Speak to them in their language."

The early scriptures were given at a time when the evolution of the world was such that people were eager for the material comfort which was obtainable then. If it had been at this time, something else would have been promised. They were told, "If you will keep from sin, then you will be amid thornless lota trees and banana trees laden with fruit, the shade of them outstretching and water flowing, and beds upraised. There shall go round them youths ever-blooming and bright ones of large eyes like pearls hidden.

There shall be created for you a new creation, and made for you
maidens young and beautiful, with gold goblets and ewers and a
cup of flowing wine. Brows ache not thereat nor the senses fail.
And fruits of what you like the best, and flesh of birds, what you
shall desire. Ye shall hear therein no vain talk nor sin, except the
cry, Peace, peace."

When a child is told, "If you do this, you shall have candy,"
however great the sacrifice is, it will do it, for it thinks, "I shall
have candy." The words in the Scriptures about the reward of
good deeds in heaven were spoken in a manner suited to the evolution of that time. The promises were made as an older person
makes promises to a child and says, "Do not take another person's
apple; I will give you another apple, even sweeter than this. Don't
take another child's doll; I will give you another doll, even better
than this."

This was the only way of keeping unevolved people from
undesirable actions.

In the same way mankind was threatened with punishment,
such as being burnt at the scorching fire, made to drink from a
fountain boiling fiercely, that there shall be no food for them but
thorns and thistles, as a mother says to her child, "You will get
a whipping if you do so."

The Prophet once said, "Hell is for the wicked, and heaven is
striven for by the fools."

Each religion has pictured heaven and hell according to familiar
scenes upon earth, in whatever part of the world it might be.

The heaven of the Hindu is an opera house. In it are the *apsaras*
and *gandharvas*, the singers and dancers, and in their hell are
snakes and scorpions, filth and worms.

In the Christian heaven the blessed become angels robed in
white, with white wings. They hold golden harps. They are in the
blue sky, seated on white clouds, singing the praise of God, and

their joy is in knowing God and in the communion of the blessed. The Christian hell is a blazing, fiery furnace and lakes of brimstone and burning sulphur, where the worm dieth not and the fire is not quenched. The devils goad the damned with the red-hot prongs of their pitchforks. They are parched with thirst, and there they remain either forever or until they have paid the debt of their sins to the uttermost farthing.

In the Moslem heaven there will be *houris* and *malayaks* to wait upon the inhabitants of *djennat*, the heavenly attendants, whose faces will be luminous and radiant with heavenly beauty and incomparably more handsome than the fair ones of the earth. Milk and honey flows in streams, and jewels and gems roll underfoot. Cooling drinks, the bracing breeze, and all fruits and delicious foods will always be ready, and fountains of *kousar*, the divine wine, will run. Every person who enters *djennat*, whether he be a child or aged, will become young. There will be the association of the holy, and the divine atmosphere will be felt all over. Hell in the Moslem traditions is said to be like a raging fire, hotter beyond comparison than any fire on the earth. There will be the association of those crying and shrieking, calling for water with flames in their mouth. Melancholy, miserable, helpless, and feeble will be the surroundings, and darkness, confusion, horror, and ignorance will be felt all around and a devilish atmosphere will overwhelm all.

One might say, "What differing accounts the different religions have given of heaven and hell." The prophets never spoke what is not true, and if we see with the philosophical view, we see that the meaning is that whatever we have idealized we shall have.

The Hindus had idealized music, singing, playing, and dancing; therefore this was their heaven.

In Christianity, because from its foundation the thought of the distinction of sex has been avoided, the holy place was held to be that where exist angels, sexless, singing to the God in the heavens above the clouds.

In Arabia, in the hot sand, every moment a person wishes for a cooling drink, and the climate makes them emotional and gives them the desire to admire youth and beauty.

Hell, in almost all religions, has been explained in some way or other as the place of torment, where all sources of torture are to be found.

The picture of heaven or hell has its origin in the simplest revelation as it comes to the mind of the prophet, a great horror at the idea of sin and a sense of joy and beauty at the sight of virtue. It takes expression first in the artistic imagery, before it comes to the lips. At once the thought of horror brings the pictures of fire, in the deserts and hot sand of Arabia especially, where water is the only rescue of the creatures, although fire is always the chief among the elements of destruction. When comes the thought of joy and beauty, it at once pictures the beauty of the opposite sex, which has charmed the soul from the first day of creation and will do the same forever. Then all delights which appeal to the senses and all sights which one longs to see, stood before his artistic view, and were expressed in the language that the listeners were capable of appreciating. While the Sufi penetrates to the source of this idea, the simple believer revels in the words.

All that the traditions say is understood by the faithful literally, but by the Sufi it is perceived differently. *Houri*s to him are the heavenly expressions of beauty appearing before the eye which was open on earth, admiring the divine immanence on earth. "God is beautiful and he loves beauty" (Koran). The whole creation was made that the beauty within the Creator might manifest in his creation, that it might be witnessed. The same tendency is working throughout the whole circuit. God's eye, through the godly on his way toward the eternal goal, sees the heavenly beauty. "No soul knows what is reserved for them of the joy of the eyes as a reward for what they have done" (Koran).

Honey is the essence of all flowers. The essence of the whole being is wisdom. Wisdom is the honey which is found in heaven. Milk is the purest and essential substance prepared in the breast of the mother. The essential sustenance of our being is the spirit, which is pure like milk, and by spirituality we drink that milk on which our soul is nourished. "Man doth not live by bread alone, but by every word that proceedeth out of the mouth of God" (Bible). The earthly treasures, such as gems and jewels, which the godly have renounced in their life upon earth, they have rolling like pebbles, worthless, beneath their feet.

To the seer, earthly wealth, which man pursues all his life long, becomes in the end as pebbles rolling under his feet. *Kousar*, wine, means the intoxicating influence of spiritual ecstasy, which is hidden in the heart as love. This purifies the mind from all impressions gathered upon it during the life on earth, thus preparing the soul for the atonement with God.

There is a different heaven and hell for each person, in accordance to the grade of his evolution. What is heaven to one person may be hell to another. A poor man will think it heaven to have a comfortable house to live in and a carriage to drive in. If a king is made to live in the house of a rich merchant, with one or two carriages, and a few servants to wait upon him, he will think it hell. A click of the tongue to the horse is more painful than ten lashes on the back of a donkey. This shows that the hell of a horse and of a donkey cannot be the same.

There is a story told of a Badishah before whom four persons were brought, arrested for one crime. He looked at one and said, "Hang him." He looked at another and said, "Life-long imprisonment." He looked at the third and said, "Banish him." He

saw the fourth; he said, "Shame! How dare you show your face
to me! Go, and never come before me again." The one who went
to be hanged killed a few more on his way to the gallows. The
exiled one went away and started his trade and roguery still more
prosperously in another country. The imprisoned one rejoiced
shamelessly with friends in the prison. But he who was relieved
from all punishment went home and committed suicide; to him
the Badishah's bitter words were worse than a bowl of poison.

It is not that God from his infinite state rewards us or punishes
us, or that there is one fold or enclosure, heaven, in which the
virtuous are allowed to be, and another arena, hell, in which all
the sinners are penned.

We experience heaven and hell in our everyday life all the time.
But here we experience both states, the dream and the physical
life. There is always the possibility of change. If we experience
hell now, tomorrow it may be heaven. If our experience today is
heaven, then there is the chance that tomorrow it may be hell.
When we go back from this world of variety we do not progress
in experience; our heaven and hell do not change much.

Let us take first the hell and heaven that each person makes for
himself here. When a person does an action with which his conscience is not pleased, the impression remains before his view,
torturing him continually and keeping before his eyes the agonies
that his self experiences. We see in the world people in high
positions, in luxurious surroundings, possessed of wealth and
power, whose evil deeds yet keep up a blazing fire within them.
Sometimes their life shows outwardly what their inward state
is; sometimes it does not, and people think that they are happy,
but they themselves find themselves in hell. And yet it is partly
covered from their eyes, for they find around them a continual
change of experience. This is the vague sight of their hell, which
they will in future experience fully.

When a person does some deed which his conscience likes, it approves him. It says, "Bravo! Well done!" His soul is glad of his deeds. In however bad environments he may be placed, still the inner joy suffices to keep him happy. When by his righteous deeds he has satisfied his conscience, the God within is pleased. However bad his worldly situation may be, he is happy within himself. The world, perhaps, may deem him unhappy, but he is happier than kings. This is his heaven.

The same experience continues uninterruptedly on the higher plane of existence, which is heaven and hell.

Every person creates his own heaven and hell.

A disciple once asked his murshid, "Pray, Murshid, let me see heaven in a vision." The murshid said, "Yes. Go into the next room, child, and sit and close your eyes and you will see heaven." The mureed went into the next room and sat in his meditation. He saw in his vision a large area but nothing else. There were not the rivers of honey and the seas of milk, nor the bricks of ruby, nor the roofs of diamonds. He went to his murshid and said, "Thank you, Murshid. Now I have seen heaven, I should like to see hell." The murshid said, "Very well; do the same again." The disciple went into the next room and sat in his meditation, and again he saw a large area, but nothing in it, no snakes, no fire, no devils nor cruel animals, nothing. He went to the murshid and said, "I saw an area, but there was nothing in it. There were not the rivers of honey nor the seas of milk, nor the roofs of diamond, nor the bricks of ruby." The murshid said, "Child, did you expect that the rivers of honey and the seas of milk would be there, or the snakes or the fire in hell? No. There is nothing there—you will have to take everything from here. This is the place to gather everything, either the delights of heaven or the fires of hell."

"Heaven is the vision of fulfilled desire, and hell the shadow of a soul on fire" (Omar Khayyam).

Our self, in reality, is heaven if blessed by divine mercy, and it is our self which is hell if cursed by the divine wrath. The seven gates spoken of in the Koran are the seven openings of our senses, through which gates we experience our heaven or hell, and the seven pinnacles mean the seven planes of man's existence, which have each its peculiar heaven and its peculiar hell.

Things appear to us as we make them appear before us. If we are tolerant with our surroundings and contented with whatever we have, enduring unavoidable discomforts and inconveniences, and if we acquire the knowledge of our being, if we see the divine immanence around us, and if we develop within us the love on which the whole world is sustained, our life becomes a preparatory heaven and our hereafter its full expression. Such is the state of the godly.

"The pious enter therein in peace and security . . . . There shall touch them therein no worry, nor shall they be cast out" (Koran).

If they are covered with rags, if lying on the dust, that dust becomes the throne of Suleiman, and their turban of rags becomes Khussrau's crown.

Our discontent with what we have in life, our intolerance of our surroundings, and lack of endurance of those conditions that we cannot avoid, our weakness in giving way to our passions and appetites, our lack of sociability, our ignorance of our true being, and our blindness to the vision of God manifest in nature, is the torment of life here and the blazing fire in the hereafter.

Heaven is for the pious whose virtues were for this end, and hell is for the wicked who himself has kindled its fire. The Sufi says, "I am beyond both, happy in the arms of the eternal peace. Neither can the joy of heaven tempt me, nor can the fire of hell touch me, for I have embraced the bliss and have kissed the curse, and have been raised above life's joys and sorrows."

Of course, no soul will remain in heaven or hell forever. It is a gradual process of dissolving in the ocean of the Eternal Being the remainder of the individual being. It is this state which is called *pulserat*, purgatory.

Kayamat, the End of the World

In introducing to you this subject I should quote the verse of a Persian poet. He says:

Thou hast hidden Thy face under the veil of Thy creation,
But I know that it is Thou who hast by one stroke set
both the worlds in motion.

The world is like a child's hoop; when a blow is given to it, it runs on and on; when the force of the blow is expired, it stops and falls down, which may be seen in all things in the world in a smaller way. When the activity of the world will have expired the world will fall down. The course of destruction is like the course of manifestation; it is in cycles. The first action is created by the blow given, and each action afterwards has caused a further action.

The course of the world's life is like that of the clock. It is wound to go for a certain time. Some clocks go for four days, some go for eight days, some you have to wind every day. When that time for which it was wound is done the wheels stop.

The law of construction and destruction may be explained as having three aspects. *Uruj*, the first aspect, shows the force of activity; *kemal* shows the climax, the limit of its progress; and *zaval* brings it back to inactivity, the end of which is the absolute *kemal*. *Kemal* shows its destructive power in both its poles, first at the end of *uruj*, the activity in force, when the progress stops, and at the finish of *zaval*, when the activity absolutely ceases. The constructive element is called *kadar*, the dominated power. The destructive is the absolute power which dominates. It is called *kazar*. All which is born, built, sprung, or made, must one day or other submit to *kazar*, the destructive power, singly or multitudinously.

It amazes us when, by an explosion, a factory is accidentally blown up, and thousands of lives are destroyed; it horrifies us to see a big city destroyed by a flood, millions of lives sacrificed—but to the Creator it amounts to nothing. It is as if a mathematician were to write a sum, multiply, add, subtract, and divide to thousands and millions of figures and suddenly take a fancy to destroy the whole thing.

There is a time when one finger is cut off, and a time when the whole hand is lost. There is a time when one limb perishes, and a time when the whole body is dead. There is a time when one thing in the room is broken, another when everything in the room is smashed, another when the whole house is ruined, another time when the whole city, or the whole country is destroyed. So there is a time when the whole world is destroyed—even the universe—but this comes in a much longer period of time.

Why is the manifestation, although it is made of eternal life, yet subject to destruction? The answer is that the eternal life is the only life and this seeming life on earth is merely an assumption.

The Prophet was once asked, what is the soul? He answered in one word, "*Umri Allah*," an action of God. There is that difference between God and his manifestation that there is between a man and his action. As the action perishes, and man remains, so the manifestation is destroyed, and God remains.

All impressions and all memory, and all stains of the world disappear from the consciousness, leaving it as pure as it was before.

If a bottle full of ink is poured into the ocean, the inky substance is absorbed, and the sea is clear and unchanged as before. When a new universe is manifested, it is manifested without the experience of a previous manifestation. When the universe has ceased to be, it starts again, and when this is repeated numberless times, it is at each time as fresh as ever.

Haunted Places

We see in our daily life the influence of the visitors who come to our house, which is felt not only in their presence but remains even after they have left. In the chair on which they have sat, the room in which they have been, the hall in which they have walked, a finer person can sense it; not, of course, everybody.

Once I had taken a room, on a journey, at Candy in Ceylon, and during the hours of my meditation in the evening, whilst I was engaged in the sacred practices, I felt very restless and wrathful, and I could not fix my mind on my meditation for a single moment. I became cross with myself, and went to bed. The uneasiness increased still more. Then I got up and wanted to look in the cupboards. I did not know why I was doing so. I think perhaps my inner self wanted to guide me to the reason of such an unusual experience with myself. I found there, to my surprise, a bunch of black hair, looking as if some woman had collected combings of hair there for a long time. I spent a bad night, and in the morning the first thing I did was to ask the landlady who had lived in this room before me. She said, "Sir, don't remind me of her. The thought of her takes my breath out of me. A woman lived here for some time. She never paid me my rent, called me bad names, fought with the men, and quarrelled every day without fail, driving away every other tenant who came to live in this house. Now my heart is at rest since she has left this house." I said, "What a shame that you gave me such a room to live in." She said, "Sir, I gave you that room on purpose, because you seem from your looks to be a godly man, so that I was sure that this room would be purified by your good influence." I had no answer for her but a smile.

If the influence of the living is such, how much greater is the influence of the dead in those places where they have lived and enjoyed life, to which they are attached, and from which death has forcibly taken them. The remembrance of their home keeps them in the home in which they lived or in the field in which they worked, and in the clubs in which they enjoyed life, and in the houses of the friends to whom they are drawn.

If the spirit, in his life, has been interested in good dishes, after his death wherever there is a good dish he will always be. If all his life he has been fond of whisky, after his death he will be at the bar where there is whisky.

The spirits are attracted also to their graves, and to the crematorium by the love of their body which they had thought their only self, which in fact was merely the instrument of experience. In fact there is not one inch of space, whether on land or on the water, free from the influence of the spirits.

A person who has been very fond of a certain society, of the society of his friends, his parents, his brothers and sisters, will long to be in that society.

The spirits that are desperately attached to this plane, and especially those among them that have but lately left it, manifest to the view as an apparition, or else by knocking at the door, by rapping on the tables and chairs, by lifting and removing objects, and by speaking. Their voice vibrates in the spheres and becomes audible to some of us. Sometimes one hears them singing, shouting, and sometimes dancing on the top floor, at times a great fighting going on among themselves. Some spirits appear to the sight of the living without any clothes, some with their legs and feet twisted outward. The former is owing to their love for lust, also to the misery they went through in life; the latter is due to their life passed in the thought of duality, and because they have gone astray in life, not having kept to the thought of unity, their body itself then demonstrates their crookedness.

I had my first experience of the spirits when a boy. One night I awoke in the midst of the night feeling a wish to look out of the window into our courtyard at the beautiful moonlight shining there. I went to the window, and looking out, I saw some way off a man of saintly appearance, clothed in a long white robe, with long snow-white hair and beard. I saw him as plainly as in full daylight. I was amazed at the sight of him, wondering how it had been possible for him to enter our courtyard, all the doors being locked. But for this saintly appearance I might have supposed him to be a thief, but the nearer he came the taller he grew. At each step his height increased, until I could no longer see his head, and as he came forward his figure became a mist, until at last he was like a shadow, and in a moment he vanished from my sight. My hair stood on end and I was completely overcome by bewilderment.

The next morning when I told my people what I had seen, they tried to make nothing of it, in order to keep me from superstitious beliefs, but others told me that they too had often seen this phantom appearing in this quarter.

This taught me that spirits are attached to those places in which they are interested, just as we are, and they are constantly attracted to the places of their interest. Their form is not solid but ethereal, and can expand.

This phantom which I saw was that of a pir who had lived in the well in our courtyard.

After a few years of these first experiences I was trying to forget and disbelieve this impression, fearing that it might lead me towards superstitions, and as I was trying to do so, one day, happening to arrive at our country cottage in the middle of the night, I found on our land a huge person at a distance of three yards from me, making a sign that he wished to wrestle with me in the way that the Indians do, who make a sign by slapping their thighs and crossing and slapping their arms, and this is a challenge. I did not for one moment take him to be a man; I at once thought that he was a spirit. I was at first terrified, comparing my size and strength with this gigantic spirit, but I had known that the spirits swallow the fearful. So although I did not know the art of wrestling, yet I determined to fight with him, and as I advanced, quite prepared to give him a box, at each step that I took forward he drew back, which naturally gave me courage to close in upon him. He retreated until he was against the wall. I was glad that now I had got him, and approaching, I struck him a strong blow, which, instead of hurting the spirit, knocked my hand against the wall, and the spirit disappeared.

The reason why the spirit appears and yet has no solid form is that it exists in a vaporous state, and the image seen in this vaporous form is nothing but the impression of his former body when on earth.

Among very many different experiences I cannot forget one which made a great impression upon my mind. I had purposely rented a haunted house in James Street, Sekunderabad, although my friends advised me not to, and in order to experience any manifestations there I slept there alone without even a servant. After a few days I began to find that whenever I played upon the veena at night, sitting on my bed, the bed would gradually begin to move as if levitating, and to rock to and fro. It would seem to rise for an instant to some height into the air, but the movement was so smooth that there was no shock. I was playing with my eyes closed, and I thought that perhaps this was the effect of the imagination under the spell of music. This went on for some time. Then I happened to send my veena to be repaired, and one night to my great horror I heard a noise as if all the windows of my house were being smashed. I got up and looked everywhere. The windowpanes were unbroken, and there was no reason to suppose that there might be anyone in the house who had caused the noise. For three days this went on and I could not sleep. I had no peace at night until my veena came back. The spirits seemed to be so much interested in my music that they rejoiced in it and showed their appreciation by lifting me up; when the food of their soul was not given they rebelled.

You might ask by what power the bed was lifted. I will say that the finer forces are much more powerful than the external forces. There is nothing that they cannot lift up or carry.

There are some who master the spirits so that the spirits bring them whatever they desire from anywhere—jewels, money, fruits, food. The spirits can even carry a person from one place to another. But those who work evil by the help of a spirit, train that spirit in evil and one day the spirit throws the bomb of evil back at them.

Sometimes spirits bring news for him who has mastered them. From whatever distance, they can bring the news in a moment of time. Sometimes the spirits go and cause trouble to someone if they are directed by the spiritualist master. I have myself seen this case. The spirits would set fire to a man's house. Sometimes his clothes would catch fire, sometimes his paper burned, sometimes the food disappeared from the dish in which it had been put and dirt was found in the dish instead.

I have myself, during twelve years' travelling throughout India, in which I concerned myself with psychical research, met with great and extremely expert spiritualists, who were able to receive news in a moment's time from any part of the world, and could even foretell future events by the help of a seer spirit.

Muhammed Chehl, a simple, unassuming man of ordinary appearance, our greatest spiritualist in India, has shown the most wonderful phenomena. He can disconnect railway carriages from a train, leaving as many as he chooses with the engine. Sometimes he has disconnected all the carriages when the train was starting, leaving the engine to start alone. He never cared to travel in any class but the third. He used often for fun to ask the people sitting in the same railway carriage to show him their tickets, and then to take the tickets, tear them up, and throw them out of the window in their presence. Everybody was angry and wanted to fight with him. He said to them, "Who has taken your tickets? You have them with you." He said to one, "Look in your turban," to another, "Look again in your pocket," to another, "See in your shoe," to another, "Find it in your sleeve." They all were amused and thought him a wonderful conjurer. He said to them: "You may think that I hid your tickets and then put them in your pockets by sleight-of-hand, but what do you think of this?" And he put his hand out of the window and asked for a few hundred tickets for Delhi, and a few hundred for Ajmir, and a few hundred for Agra, and he asked them what other stations they wanted. When the train reached the next station there was great excitement. The station master had just received a telegram from the last station saying that all the tickets for those stations had been stolen in one second's time and nobody knew where they had gone. Muhammed Chehl never did such phenomena unless he wanted to amuse himself. He never cared for notoriety or money. Nothing would induce him to take a show or a trade of his power. If he had cared to show his great power in the Western world, he would have filled his house with bags of gold.

Spiritualism

The believers in spirit phenomena many times lose their balance and go to such lengths that the pursuit of spiritualism becomes a craze with them, as it is always interesting to tell and to listen to ghost stories. The teller has a tendency to exaggerate the story to make it more interesting and to excite the astonishment of the hearer, and a simple listener has a tendency, sometimes, to take the rod for a snake.

There is a well-known case which happened in India where among friends ghosts were being discussed. One among them said, "I don't believe in such things. I can go and sit half the night in the graveyard, if you like." The friend said, "They will not believe you unless you do so." He went the same night to sit in the graveyard. Half the night he passed avoiding all the threats that his imagination produced before him during that dark night in the graveyard. When the time was over, as he started to return to his friends, his long robe caught in some thorns growing there. He thought surely the spirit had caught him. He fell down and was choked with fear, and in the morning he was found dead.

Many times the enemies of landlords spread rumors that the house is haunted, so that they may not be able to get a tenant. Sometimes the pretended spiritualists, who have made this their life's occupation, make it as interesting a play as they can, by arranging some knocks from here and there, by lifting the chairs and tables by means of an arrangement of wires, by producing effects of light and shade by means of phosphorus; they take advantage of the simple-minded. Some pretend to bring and carry messages from the spirit or to the spirit and dupe many earnest inquirers into these matters. Many carry out their questionable purposes by holding spirit meetings. All this drives material people, unbelievers in the spirit, still further away from the know-ledge of the finer existence, and makes the so-called spiritualists so much engrossed in their hobby that the time never comes in their life when they realize their own spirit.

In ordinary life we experience two planes: the physical plane, in which we experience by the eyes, the ears, and all the organs of the body; and the mental plane, the plane of thought and feeling. When we are asleep and all our organs are resting, we see our-selves just as we appear when waking, in various surroundings. This shows us that we have another being besides this physical being and other eyes besides these eyes. Whilst we are dreaming, the dream is real to us. When we awake, we think, "I was there and now I am here. If what I saw in the dream had been real, it must all still be here, now that I am awake, but it is all gone." We distinguish the dream as a dream by the contrast of the waking condition.

Whilst we are dreaming, if someone comes and tells us that it is a dream, it is not real, we shall not believe him. Or now, if some-one tells us it is a dream, we shall say, "No, it is quite real, I see the things about me." There is an expression we use of what is passed, saying, "It is all a dream now."

When the person after his death still longs for the earthly joys, his condition is very bad, because he has not the physical body with which to experience them. He is like a cricketer or a football player who has lost his arms—he longs to play, but he has no

arms; or a singer whose throat has been operated on—he will long
to sing, but he cannot because his throat is gone.

When the physical plane is taken from a person, then the dream
remains as reality, because there is no contrast to prove it otherwise, and this state of existence is called *missal*. He cannot
experience upon the earth now because he has lost the physical
means. All the impressions that he has gathered upon earth are
his world. It is the nature of the mind to gather as many impressions as it can. From this store the pictures that he sees are
formed. We do not dream of what we do not know, of what we
have not seen. The butcher sees the meat all day, and at night he
does not dream of the dairy but of meat.

Sometimes not only here but also in the East, those apparitions
of the departed that come to communicate, to warn, to speak with
someone dear to them, are called spirits. Really the word is in-
appropriate. The spirit is the essence, the soul that swells beyond.
But since the word is used, let us take it. These so-called spirits
are not the soul alone, but the soul together with the mind, that is,
all that remains of the external self after the death of the body.

Sometimes the ghosts so much wish to experience the life of this
world that to a certain extent they make themselves substantial.
They cannot make themselves as concrete as we are. If so, they
could live here. But to a certain extent they do, by actionizing the
elements around, either the ether or the air.

When people see a ghost, it is in part illusion and in part they
may really see. When the inner eye sees, these outer eyes think
that they see. But if they try to touch the ghost, there is nothing
there.

You may say, "The actual self of the spirit might show itself in
the mist, but where does he get the clothes in which he appears,
or anything that he may hold in his hand?" The answer is that it is
the impression of itself that the spirit holds which mirrors in the

soul of the spectator, so that by his concrete illusion he feels its presence as positively as if he saw it with his own eyes.

The dead feel the thought, the good wish of the living. Prayer and religious rite focus the mind of the living with that of the dead, so that the dead may be helped by the living, or the living may be blessed by a holy spirit.

The custom of offering food, perfume, or incense to the dead exists among Hindus and Moslems. If someone comes to see us and we set food before him, or luncheon, or whatever may please him, it is all the better. It is so with the dead also. They enjoy by our eating, by our smelling the perfume, because, although they do not enjoy the actual thing that we put upon the table before them, yet the impression of our mind, the joy of the thing, mirrors itself upon their soul.

The dead person becomes more interested in the things that speak to the mind than in the material satisfactions. Therefore when the food and drink and perfume are offered, the sacred names, the Surahs of the Koran, are read before them that their intelligence may be satisfied also.

In order to know of the existence of the spirit we must ourselves live in the spirit, above the matter. If a person loses someone whom he loved very much and in whom he was quite absorbed, and he goes about lost in the thought of that person, he will become dead to the world around him, and then wherever he goes, in the crowds, in the jungles, he feels the presence of that person, because his self is no more before his view.

Our connection with the beings upon earth is much greater, because we are conscious of our earthly life. We think of our friends whom we see, and sympathize with them, but we think much less of those who have passed and what their condition may be now. Those who are living on other planes also think much less of us. There may be a connection between a mother and a child, or between a lover and his beloved, but ordinarily there is no contact between the living and the dead.

This is a subtle subject. In speaking of it, I must say that it is better to have our connection more with the beings living upon earth than to have the craze to meet with the people on the other side of life. It is here that we are meant to evolve, and by being absorbed in those who have passed away we are taken away from the life we are meant to have, and then we live on earth as dead. People in pursuit of the spirit show on their face the dead expression.

To have a devotion for the immortal and holy beings who have passed is allowable because they are alive, more than the living and more than the dead.

There are spirits whom we attract by our love for them, by our wish for their presence. We are surrounded in life by our friends, by those whom we like, whom by our liking we attract to us. And the spirits also we attract by our love. These are usually of a higher sort, those whom we call upon for help, for guidance, the murshids, the prophets.

There are the visions of the murshids, the higher beings. These come to the initiate. They come to guide, to help in all difficulties. Someone who is quite absorbed in the thought of a prophet or murshid may be so lost in him that if he calls upon the prophet or murshid in any difficulty, he upon whom he calls will always come and help him.

To have devotion for a murshid or a prophet who has passed is better than to ask for his help in whatever difficulty we may be, for God Almighty is closest to us and sufficient to help us in all our difficulties. No mediation of anyone, living or spirit, is necessary. Of course, as in life we depend upon each other's help, so in the higher plane also if the help of some holy spirit is granted to us, we may have it, and if God's being is realized in all, from whichever source the help comes it is from God.

I have had many experiences of the vision of my murshid. If I were to tell you all of them I could speak for many hours, but I will tell you one, when making a three days' journey through the jungle, in a place where there was great danger from robbers, and every night two or three travellers were killed. Ours was the smallest caravan. Generally the caravans were of twenty wagons, but it happened that ours was of three wagons. And I had with me very precious gems given by the Nizam of Hyderabad, of great value, and instead of arms I had musical instruments with me. All the night I saw the form of my murshid, at first faint, afterwards distinct, walking with the wagon. The two other wagons were attacked and robbed. A few worthless bundles were taken. My wagon was safe.

And not this one instance only, but a thousand experiences of the sort I have had in life.

The animals can see the spirits more than we, because their activity is less than ours. We, owing to the worries and anxieties of life and the comforts and temptations of earth, are more on the surface, although our intelligence is brighter than the animals. Animals after their death also appear as spirits, but for a less period and less in number than the human beings, for they are not absorbed in the earthly life so much as man is in his person and possessions.

I once had an experience with a dog. Returning from the theatre in the middle of the night with a few friends, I saw a dog following us. He showed an especial interest in us. One of us, considering it to be a street dog, struck it with his stick. The moment that the stick hit him, the dog disappeared, and at the same moment the stick broke in pieces. This happened in the presence of many people. We then found that a dog, a pet of our family, very fond of us, had died six months before, and it was the spirit of that dog, still attached to us, that was following. This dog was an exceptional one; one remarkable thing about him was that every Thursday, regularly, he would fast.

Obsession

We often find in our daily life that we do things that we do not wish to do, things against our will and contrary to our ideals. Sometimes we recognize that such or such a friend has induced us to do an action which otherwise we should not have done, and we ascribe to him the credit or discredit of its result. It may be because our love for him is so great that we take his word to heart, whether we agree with it or not, or we may be so situated under the power of another that we cannot but act as he wishes.

Sometimes we feel inclined to do a thing which apparently we have no reason to do. This is owing to the silent influence of some other person acting upon us without any spoken word and causing us to do that which we imagine to be his wish.

Sometimes the thoughts and conditions of mind of another person make so strong an impression upon us, either in the presence of that person or in his absence, according to the extent of his power, that his condition is transferred to us. We sometimes laugh without reason on seeing the intensity of another person's laughter, and we feel sad without any reason when we are in contact with one who is sorrowful. We fulfill the wish of another, not knowing that he had any such wish, sometimes even without his knowledge of it.

It sometimes happens that one feels a desire to eat fish, and finds that the cook has prepared the very dish of which one was thinking; sometimes we think of a friend and it happens that the friend comes to see us.

All such instances are proofs of silent suggestion, the inner influence directed consciously or unconsciously. Sometimes we are under the influence of another person's mind and thought, at another time another may be under our influence; it depends upon the positive and negative state of will.

Suggestions are of two kinds: spoken command, and suggestion by thought. *Sahibidil*, the powerful minded, often does not intentionally command or suggest, and yet every word spoken by the powerful and thought by the master mind is fulfilled. "Word spoken and action done," which accomplishment is called *siddhi* by Yogis, and those so accomplished are called *sahibidil* among Sufis.

Hypnotism and mesmerism are a kind of obsession in the presence for either a good or a bad purpose.

The black magicians work six different spells: murder, fascination, severance, unrest, torture, persecution. The same are also wrought by the evil soul whose occupation it is still to work evil upon earth. This it accomplishes by the sole means of obsession. Those subject to its influence experience any of these ill effects.

All this is partial obsession. Thousands of such influences come and go like moving pictures upon the blank curtain of man's mind, and it rarely happens that the effect lasts longer; it is then that people call it obsession.

The influence of the dead is the same as the influence of the living, and even more. Their spirit throws its reflection upon the mirror of man's mind, and man acts as the spirit wishes, knowing all the while that his wishes are other than the spirit's. The intensity of spirit obsession is much greater than that of the influence of a living person, for the living are themselves subject to influences and obsessions, and their own self is an obsession to them, reflecting the diverse pictures of their own life upon their soul; but the spirits, from whom the burden of external existence is taken, are much more powerful and freer and more inclined to obsess others.

Many times a crime is committed by a man under the influence of another. A person with a bad thought of revenge, the desire to kill somebody, by the very concentration of his evil thought becomes so weak that he cannot do it himself. Then he may consciously or unconsciously by the intensity of his desire convey to some other person the suggestion to do it. The other person is innocent of the evil desire and so has the strength to accomplish it. This is often seen with the anarchists; among anarchists there are some who plan the deed only and there are others who carry it out.

There are two sorts of obsession: one is when one soul imparts its qualities to another; the other is when one soul causes another to accomplish some deed; this may be either evil or good.

In India we have often seen this with the snakes. The soul focuses itself upon the snake, and then the snake will feel an inclination to go and bite the person.

If the influence is so strong from a living person, the obsession of a dead person, of a spirit, is much stronger still. The dead has no other means of expression, and so he seizes upon a weak person, a weak mind, and controls that.

It is not that the soul enters into the body—the soul is much too large to do that; but it mirrors itself upon the other soul. A spirit focuses itself upon the soul of another; the greater power holds the lesser.

If a man has left this world full of anger, full of hatred against his enemy, and longing to do him harm, he cannot be peaceful. If a person leaves the earth with revengeful feelings he will long to accomplish his revenge. He is restless and looking for some means to accomplish his desire. The negative soul, suited for his purpose, receives this impression—not the positive soul, but one who is weak bodily or in mind. The well-balanced and vigorous throw off such influences; they are not easily affected.

For a good purpose or for an evil purpose a spirit may obsess.

If a mother dies before she has been able to bring her child up, and all her thoughts and affection are centered in the child, she may obsess. Then some one of the relations will feel inclined to take the child and do all he can for it.

It may happen in the case of soul mates. Especially in the East this is often seen, where a man loves a girl or a woman whom he has seen once and there is no chance of his seeing her ever again. Then, if he dies, she may become obsessed. She can think of nothing else than of his thought and she becomes half dead, and is often in a trance. It may not be that she loved him very much, but his thought obsesses her, and she feels his condition only.

The disciples of Khaja Nizam-ud-din Wali, a great saint of Delhi, were once sitting waiting for him to come to speak upon a very abstruse and difficult matter, when to their astonishment they saw his servant come into the room and sit down on the murshid's seat.

Khaja Nizam-ud-din Wali then came in, made a very deep bow to the servant and took his seat before him. The servant began to speak and spoke for some time, explaining some very subtle and deep questions. Then a change came over his face, he looked around, and ran from the room in great confusion. Khaja Nizam-ud-din Wali then told his disciples that he had asked his murshid for the answer to some very difficult question, and that the subject was so complex that the murshid needed a human form in order to explain it exactly, and he had therefore spoken through the servant.

I have taken a great interest in this subject. As a boy, from curiosity, I studied it very much. I have always gone where obsessed people could be seen and I have seen some very curious things. I have myself seen two very remarkable cases of obsession.

One was in a Parsi family. There was a young lady who sometimes once in a day and sometimes two or three times would change her mood and would speak in Arabic and Persian, and she spoke of philosophy and metaphysics, which she had never been taught. She was so strongly obsessed that she did not care to speak with her father and mother or her brothers and sisters or with anyone, nor would she ever go out. She always had incense burning in her room and led a very retired life. They brought learned people to speak with her, and she discussed with them like a great philosopher and got the better of the argument. Then she would forget it all again.

At Sekunderabad there was a boy who sang the Telagu songs. He had never learnt them, because Telagu is not spoken there among Moslems. Sometimes he would begin to sing and sing many songs, and then afterwards he could not sing one.

Many people who are obsessed go to be healed to the tomb of a Sufi, Miran Datar, at Unjha in Central India, a saint who in his lifetime cured cases of obsession and continued doing so even after death. I once visited this place. On the steps of the tomb there was a man sitting who seemed a quiet and thoughtful person. He was engaged in his prayers. I spoke to him. If I had known that he was obsessed, really I would not have spoken to him, but I did not know it. I asked him, "Why are you here?" He said, "Do not ask me such a question." I said, "Why not?" He said, "Because I am afraid. Now that I am near this holy tomb I have a little strength to answer you; if I were not here I could not even do that." He told me that he had been a store-keeper on some British liner going up and down between Bombay and London. One day at sea he felt a strange feeling, as if some power were taking hold of him, and he was not able to do anything. He wanted to go to eat, but he could not go. After that many times this power would take hold of him, and he could not do what he wanted to do. At times he wanted to eat but could not. At other times, when he did not want to eat he had to go and eat. And he became quite weak. He told the ship's doctor, but the doctor could do nothing for him. Then he went to see many doctors, but they could not help him. At last he went to the tomb of Miran Datar to see if he could find a little relief.

Whilst I was at the tomb of Miran Datar, there came the Prince of Khairalu, a very handsome boy of twelve or thirteen, accompanied by aides-de-camp and attendants. He was brought there to be cured. A conversation began of which we could hear only the part spoken by the prince as words of the spirit that obsessed him. He said, "I will not leave him. I like him so much. He was in the forest, shooting, and he came near the tree on which I was sitting. Don't whip me, Miran, I am his guardian. I will not leave him. Miran, don't whip me." The prince began to run, leaping high into the air, and showed every sign of being severely whipped. He ran round and round the tomb, leaping every time that the invisible whip struck the spirit. At last he fell down exhausted, and his attendants at once lifted him up and carried him away.

When I came to the Western world I was curious to know whether it is only we in the East who have so many obsessed people, or whether there are obsessed people in the West also. They said to me, "Here if someone were to show such a condition, we should put him in the lunatic asylum. If you wish to see such cases as you explain you must go there." I went, and found that there were many who were mad and many also who were obsessed. I wanted to try some experiments of casting out the influence, but the doctors would not let me, because they wanted a medical diploma, which unfortunately I lacked.

Then they took me into the laboratory where they were dissecting brains, and they showed me that this one had this spot in his brain decayed and therefore he was mad, and this man had that cavity in his skull and therefore his career was so. I asked them whether it was the decay that caused the madness, or the madness that caused the decay? At first they were astonished, but then they thought that there might be something in my philosophy.

According to the mystic's view mostly the cause is within. It is the fever that gives heat, not the heat that gives fever. It is not that the weeping is first and then the sadness comes. The sadness comes first and causes the tears to fall.

An Arab who had lost his camel, after searching for it everywhere, heard that it was in the stable of the Sherif of Mekkah. He went to the Sherif and said, "I have been told that my she-camel which I lost has been sold to you and is in your stable." The Sherif asked him, "How will you recognize your camel? Has she any particular marks?" The Arab said in answer, "She has two black marks upon her heart." The Sherif was amazed to hear this, wondering how the Arab should know about his camel's heart, and in order to ascertain the truth, the camel was cut open, and two black marks were found upon her heart. The Sherif asked, "How could you know that your camel had these two black marks upon her heart?" The Arab replied, "My camel twice was in great sorrow; twice she lost her foal; she looked up and gave a deep sigh, and I knew that each time a black mark was left upon her heart."

I have seen that in the West there are many suffering under such influences, but, science being the conqueror of religion, the casting out of spirit influences written of in the Bible is today no more than a superstition to many.

The East, on the contrary, has gone to the other extreme. There are there a great many cases of illness which are taken to the casters-out of devils, and these, in order to get as many patients as they can, interpret every disease as the influence of a spirit. There are, however, two benefits in this course, one being that the patient thinks that it is not a disease in his self, but an external influence which can pass away if cast out; and instead of his taking the anxiety of his sickness so much to heart that the impression itself of having a disease whose root is in the body leads him quickly to death, in this case, however serious the illness may be, the patient's impression is, "It is a spirit; it will be cast out," and this restores him to health. The other benefit is that a wise person who casts out the spirits can by this pretense arouse in the patient an excitement, as the fakirs generally do, until he begins to confess his heart's disease, some hidden thought or feeling, which may have made him so ill, though he could not utter it, being constrained by the situation in which he may be placed, and when this poison has been brought out, the patient can easily be cured. There are sometimes women who, owing to the strict customs and manners of their country and religion, cannot tell the secret of their despair to anyone, and thus they hold the poisonous seed in their heart until their death, and this eats them within. Many have longings which could not be attained, many have jealous fits which could not be explained, many have heart-breaks which could not be repaired. All such cases show externally a bodily disease, which doctors try to cure by chemical prescriptions, while the root lies there notwithstanding, which treatment is like poison within mixed with poison without. The result is, without any doubt, death.

As soon as the patient's secret is known to the healer, he has really made a successful operation in the invisible heart and taken out all the poisonous substance which was causing the sickness and leading the patient to his death. He then releases him from that by words of consolation, by fragrance, by music, by the recitation of the names of God, and by mirroring upon the heart of the obsessed his own wisdom and piety.

Of course, there are very few, even in the East, who would give the right treatment, but mostly there are real devils amongst those who profess to cast out devils.

I have known good and bad, sin and virtue, right and wrong; I have judged and have been judged; I have gone through birth and death, joy and pain, heaven and hell; and what I realize in the end is that I am in all and all is in me.

Index